FRONT LINE MISSION

'Hullo!
I just happened
to be passing

FRONT LINE MISSION

Ministry in the Market Place

by

DENIS CLARINGBULL

Illustrations by Ray Price

The Canterbury Press
Norwich

First published 1994 by The Canterbury Press Norwich
(a publishing imprint of Hymns Ancient & Modern Limited,
a registered charity)
St Mary's Works, St Mary's Plain,
Norwich, Norfolk, NR3 3BH

British Library Cataloguing in Publication Data

A catalogue record for this book is available
from the British Library

ISBN 1–85311–081–7

Typeset by Datix International Limited
Bungay, Suffolk and
Printed and bound in Great Britain by
St Edmundsbury Press Limited
Bury St Edmunds, Suffolk

Foreword

DENIS CLARINGBULL has over thirty years' experience of supporting Christians who work in 'the front line', mainly in commerce and industry. As an Industrial Chaplain he has come into close contact with those who face the challenges of the Gospel in their work situation. Denis, however, has not lost contact with traditional Anglican parochial structures; he has combined his Industrial Chaplaincy with support for a church and congregation within inner city Birmingham. He knows the tensions that exist betwen maintenance and mission, but he argues for those who are on the front line to be supported by the wider Church.

Sometimes he is critical of the Church as an institution, but his approach in this book is always practical and helpful.

I commend this book to all who are concerned for those who are on the front line of the Church's mission, especially as the Decade of Evangelisation continues to challenge us all.

+ Mark
BISHOP OF BIRMINGHAM

September 1993

Contents

ACKNOWLEDGEMENTS

It was Peter Morgan, present Director General of the Institute of Directors who inspired me to write this book. He it was who first drew my attention to the plight of lay people who, though expected to resource the Institutional Church, received very little in the way of practical resource for their own day-to-day secular tasks 'at the front line'!

The Diocese of Birmingham (to whom this book is dedicated) made it possible for me to study this problem during a sabbatical leave in California in 1991. On my return, a combination of surgery and a motor car accident (which involved an extended spell of hospitalisation) provided the space to type the manuscript.

I am aware that I have taken a 'broad brush' approach and I acknowledge my debt to numerous people for what I have written.

My thanks, in particular, are due to the Reverend Michael Dunk and Kay Miller for checking the script, and the Reverend Ray Price for his humorous illustrations. Without their patient and devoted assistance this book could not have been written!

Special acknowledgement is due to Rachel Jenkins of the William Temple Foundation and to The Canterbury Press Norwich for allowing me to quote from the many hymns taken from *Hymns Ancient and Modern (Revised)* that I have used throughout this book.

DENIS CLARINGBULL
Birmingham, November 1993

CHAPTER ONE

Introduction: Support the Front line!

A Military Analogy

In times of war, those in the front line have a crucial role. This is true whether it be the pilots who fly the aircraft, the troops on the ground, or the men and women at sea. They bear the brunt of the battle. This is not to minimise the important role of those in 'Command HQ'. Yet if those back at base fail to be sensitive to the real needs of those in the front line, and if they do not supply the front line troops with the equipment they need, the battle will not be won.

This is an analogy. Like all analogies it is dangerous to stretch it too far. The point I wish to make is that Christian lay people (not the clergy) are the 'front line' of the Christian Church.

The Front Line – Public Life

The task of Christian lay people is to 'live the gospel' in their day-to-day lives in the secular world. Their 'front line' is their daily secular occupation ... in the world of business and commerce, the professions, the community, as well as in their family life. This is what lay ministry is all about. Indeed this IS lay ministry. It is the job of the clergy and hierarchy of the Church to affirm support and equip lay people in the front line task of their public life as well as in their domestic and private life.

Sadly, lay people often complain that they do not receive that support from the Church. Business people, for example, who grapple with ethical problems in their businesses, sometimes feel abandoned by the Church. The Church frequently appears unable to comprehend their problems or offers facile solutions. Worship seems irrelevant. What happens in church on Sunday seems to bear little or no relationship to the reality of Monday morning.

However, the Church does appear to want lay people to prop up ecclesiastical structures. The Church appeals to commerce and industry for funds to maintain its buildings. People who earn their living as accountants are frequently asked by clergy to become church treasurers in their spare time. Lay people are asked to spend a lot of time in church buildings talking about church matters. Yet these discussions seldom relate to the day-to-day experiences of lay people in their 'front line' occupations. Moreover these tasks which the institutional church sometimes asks of its members frequently divert the energies of lay people away from their secular task, often placing additional burdens upon them. How often does one hear the groan, 'What? Another meeting? That means I am out every night this week!'

Need for Support

Deep down, business people (particularly if they are Christians) cry out for support from the Church as they grapple with their day-to-day decisions. They pray. They receive the sacraments. But they also say that they need practical support and advice in relating their day-to-day business experiences to relevant insights of the Gospel. They need opportunities to be able to 'tell their story . . .' The clergy are often ill-equipped for this task or may have other priorities and pre-occupations. Frequently ordained ministers themselves are under stress and are unable to cope with what is seen as yet one more demand on their time!

People in the 'front line' of public life are liable to experience stress as they grapple with the decisions that they are called on to make day by day. Business decisions often involve ethical criteria.

Should we break the law and open our shops on a Sunday? Should we make all these people redundant? Should we allow his takeover to go forward? For similar reasons those in trade unions, in government and in the professions face ethical dilemmas.

Wider Issues

There are also wider issues. Some of the most important questions concern the future role of industry – what are the principles that should underpin the functions of industry? What relationship should there be between the world of business and commerce and with government? What relationship should there be between industry and the local community, its shareholders, employees and customers? Industry does not operate in a moral vacuum. There are ethical criteria in investment policies and advertising practices. There are the implications for business resulting from closer integration with mainland Europe. There are questions of employee discrimination and the responsibility of companies towards the environment.

There will be those who say that these matters have nothing to do with the Church. There are those who would say that these matters are to be left to market forces or political expediency. They are not supposed to be within the realms of religion. Christianity should be concerned with what is individual, private, and spiritual. The Church should concentrate upon the task of 'saving souls'.

Yet if the Church took that advice, deep thinking Christians working in the 'front line' would feel abandoned altogether.

The Church does not abandon troops in battle. Chaplains in the armed services are alongside them in the front line. Their ministry is deeply appreciated by the troops. For similar reasons the Church appoints Industrial Chaplains to support lay people in their 'front line' secular occupations. The ministry of Industrial Chaplains is also deeply appreciated, though alas, sometimes misunderstood by the Church.

It has to be said that Industrial Chaplains themselves have their problems. So do other sector ministers who are perceived to be specialist and who do not appear to make a financial contribution to the life of the institutional churches! Very often the Church fails to understand the importance of their work. Chaplains frequently have to defend the work they do, particularly if they are full time and suspected of being a drain on Church funds! Industrial Chaplains are often asked to take on the additional responsibilities of looking after a church congregation in the traditional way.

Anglican Industrial Chaplains are encouraged to become vicars, but even the smallest parishes have church buildings which (particularly if they are ancient) make their own unique demands on time and energy.

It is important to examine these issues during the Decade of Evangelism. Statistics seem to indicate that all the main stream churches are in decline. If present trends continue, the dwindling congregations will be composed almost entirely of retired people. Those engaged in commerce, industry, the professions and other aspects of secular institutional life will continue to drift away. It is interesting to note that those churches which DO attract business people in growing numbers are mainly 'evangelical' churches. These churches do encourage lay people to 'tell their story' and to bear witness to the way that Jesus Christ is alongside them in their secular lives. 'Prayer breakfasts' for business people are becoming very popular. Yet the evangelical approach (which can be divisive and exclusive) is not to everybody's taste. There are other ways than 'prayer breakfasts' to empower lay people in their secular ministry. Moreover 'prayer breakfasts' are sometimes more concerned with piety than with public and economic policy.

Worlds Apart

Sometime ago a questionnaire was circulated by the churches in Surrey and Hampshire to industrial and commercial companies and also to local churches of various denominations. It was an attempt to survey how those who work in business and commerce see the Church and how the Church perceives local business. The report of that survey is entitled *Worlds Apart*.

Most of the companies in that area replied that they were motivated by profit, success and survival. The creation of wealth came out as a dominant goal. Whilst several firms expressed 'benevolence' towards the Church, the overwhelming opinion was that there is no place for the Church in the sphere of economic life, except possibly in connection with personal morality or personal domestic problems which affect the businessperson's 'performance'. The outstanding impression in the survey is of a huge gap between the world of economic activity and the churches. The world of business and the world of the Church were perceived as 'worlds apart'.[1]

Similarly the churches seemed to perceive commerce and industry either as a source of funds for various appeals, a source of annoyance (as when there are problems of pollution, etc) or a target to attack when commercial interests seem to outweigh ethical criteria.

Hopefully a different result would be obtained in an area with a long history of effective Industrial Mission.

Bridge-Building

If the *Worlds Apart* report is to be taken seriously in the Decade of Evangelism it would seem that a lot of 'bridge-building' remains to be done. The Christian Gospel proclaims how Jesus became incarnate in the front line in a carpenter's workshop in Palestine two thousand years ago, and that the Church is called to be the Body of Jesus Christ incarnate in the workshops of the world today. The Church must not therefore behave as if it were a private holy club for religious people, or a safe refuge from the 'naughty' world. The Church proclaims God's love for the whole world. The focus of the Church's ministry should therefore be to those who are engaged in the secular world and to provide support and affirmation to those who are in the 'front line' in public life.

This book will explore practical ways of giving this support and enquire what new resources may be needed. It will explore liturgy and worship, spirituality and counselling, and look at some of the ethical dilemmas that people encounter. It will delve into theology and investigate the training that may be required by lay people as they grapple with their front line tasks and examine stress at work and see the immense influence that institutions have in shaping the values and behaviour of those who work within them.

This book is an introduction to the kinds of issues which must be faced if the churches are to offer more effective support to lay people at the front line in the Decade of Evangelism.

CHAPTER TWO

Ministry in the Market Place

A Sabbatical Experience

During a sabbatical in California, USA in 1991, I stayed at the Church Divinity School of the Pacific in Berkeley, not far from San Francisco. This Episcopal Theological College is twinned with Cuddesdon Theological College near Oxford, England. It is part of a consortium of theological colleges of all denominations sharing central library facilities and closely linked with the magnificent campus of the University of California in Berkeley. The colleges are also linked to various secular consortia dealing with matters relating to business ethics and social policy in the San Francisco Bay area.

I was there during the period July–September 1991. I was able to participate in various 'ad hoc' courses which seemed relevant. The most significant of these was conducted by Professor Robert Bellah, author of the American best seller *Habits of the Heart* an important book which analyses American society. I was present at a seminar preceding the launching of another of his books entitled *The Good Society*.

Halfway through my sabbatical the ordinands returned to the college. One of the first sessions of the new term was on

Lay Ministry chaired by the College Dean. The Dean asked the new students about their experience of Lay Ministry. The replies were many and various. Some had been Sunday School teachers, servers, acolytes, lay readers, lay preachers and lay pastors. The Dean received all the replies without comment. It took a considerable time before it dawned on the group that there was more to Lay Ministry than this! Had they not exercised any ministry in any previous employment? Had not some of the students been bankers, business people, teachers and broadcasters? Did they not exercise a ministry in those capacities?

Unfortunately, however, when I interviewed the Dean I discovered that the college syllabus made very little provision at any depth to amplify this wider concept of lay ministry nor what the implications would be for the ministry of the clergy if lay ministry were to be taken really seriously!

The term 'Lay Ministry' frequently conjures up in our minds the kind of ministry described by those students. I went into the bookshop of Grace Cathedral, San Francisco and looked on the bookshelves at the section labelled 'Lay Ministry'. The books on display were all about the ministry of acolytes, Youth Leaders, Sunday School Teachers, etc. Even the General Theological Union bookshop in Berkeley carried similar titles under this heading. I did not find it easy to locate books on authentic Lay Ministry in the secular world. However I did find one such book and I commend it for study. It is entitled *The Monday Connection*.

The Monday Connection

The Monday Connection is written by a layman, William Diehl, who spent most of his life as Sales Manager for the Bethlehem Steel Corporation. The author describes his experience as a young member of his Lutheran Congregation:

'My Pastor made frequent references to Luther's affirmation of the universal priesthood of the baptized. We were all to serve as intermediaries between God and other humans. Yet I saw absolutely no way which I served as priest in my Monday world.'[1]

William Diehl goes on to explain how 'other messages' came through to him quite clearly from his pastor and local congregation. He was made to feel uncomfortable if he missed a church committee meeting because of a business commitment. His pastor used the image of 'businessman' to illustrate evil practice. Diehl describes how he received affirmation for his work as a Sunday School teacher and Youth Adviser and he received training for these tasks, but he received no affirmation and no training for his work as a Christian in business.

He says:

'For a number of years I lived in two worlds, the Sunday world of religion and the Monday world of secularism.'[2]

This cry echoes similar experiences in Britain today. In spite of numerous books such as *God's Frozen People* written many years ago, the Church seems unable to grasp the reality of the importance of Lay Ministry.

Some British Examples

The Chief Executive of a major city in the West Midlands echoed this cry when he gave the Address at the City's Annual Industrial Festival in 1990. He said:

'I see little evidence of a community of support where I work which could strengthen me. Almost the reverse, for often there seems to be an echo of the Sunday-Family-Church routine in the issues that the Church wishes to address. We need to define a positive role for the Church in work and in working for our City Harvest.'

Peter Morgan, Director General of the Institute of Directors made a similar plea. He described how his country church involved him in all kinds of 'churchy' activities but did not really offer informed support for his secular task.

I recall meeting a very senior director of a multi-national company who at that time, was looking forward to his retirement. He said that he could then give much more of his time to the Church. I knew what he meant but I found myself thinking what a pity it was that he did not seem to make the connection between his task as a responsible Christian lay person and his role as a director of that company. But then, we must also ask whether his parish church encouraged him to do so!

This is not to diminish the important work that lay people do undertake for the Christian Church in other ways. One has only to call to mind the profound importance of the lay preacher in the Methodist tradition. The former Speaker of the House of Commons, George Thomas, is an outstanding lay preacher, who speaks from the depths of the experience of one brought up in the poverty and hard work of a Welsh mining village.

George Thomas is a supreme example of a lay preacher who can 'tell his story' and relate his Christian convictions to his life's experience and inspire his hearers in a marvellous way. He is also a supreme example of a Christian lay person in the front line of public life who, as Mr Speaker, saw very clearly the connections between Sunday and Monday. Mr Speaker Thomas grappled with the most demanding and complicated decisions, maintaining throughout his neutral position as Speaker in the House of Commons. I once had the privilege of meeting George Thomas in The Speaker's House, and that is an experience I shall never forget.

George Thomas was keenly aware of the need for support groups. In his book *Mr Speaker*, he describes how he welcomed such groups to meet in his official residence.

'They did not want specialist Bible Study and prayer. They simply wanted to talk to each other in a Christian setting.'[3]

Later in this book there is a chapter devoted to stories from the front line as lay people describe their experience in politics, industry, commerce and the professions.

The issues faced by lay people in public life have become very complex in recent years, particularly in industry and commerce. Changes in technology and ideology have brought new pressures upon Christians in public life.

This concern was expressed by the William Temple Foundation in 1986:

'We are concerned about new pressures on Christians emerging in industrial and commercial organisations and in the public sector. Lay people caught in these frontier situations need support and sustenance at an individual level if they are to be obedient to the distinctive value systems of the Christian faith. But even more so do they need help and encouragement if they attempt to carry those values into the very heartland of industrial, commercial and public life, so that the value systems, practices and policies of our institutions show signs of transformation, as well as the lives of ordinary people.'

This latter point needs to be underlined. Christianity is concerned as much with transforming the lives of institutions as with transforming the lives of individuals. It is too simplistic to say that institutions are transformed by transforming individuals 'one by one'.

St Paul says:[4]

'In Christ everything in heaven and on earth was created, not only things visible but also the invisible orders of thrones, sovereignties, authorities and powers: the whole universe has been created through him and for him. He exists before all things, and all things are held together in him. He is the head of the body, the Church. He is its origin, the first to return from the dead to become in all things supreme. For in him God in all his fullness chose to dwell, and through him to reconcile all things to himself, making peace through the shedding of his blood on the cross . . . all things, whether on earth or in heaven.'

All things, all institutions, all authorities, all powers, in heaven and on earth, can be transformed by Christ.

The values and beliefs to which Christians are committed are increasingly being challenged, often by the policies of the organisations within which they work. For example, Christians have long held that Sunday is a special day of rest and recreation. It is a day to worship God and to be with the family. Yet many large supermarkets began to flout Sunday trading laws. Christian and Jewish leaders sent a joint statement to the Prime Minister in 1991 which stated: 'It is surely wholly unacceptable for those who seek profit by illegal action to pursue it without censure.'

In December 1993, Members of Parliament voted for a partial de-regulation which allowed large stores to trade for six hours each Sunday. The Archbishop of Canterbury expressed his deep concern that there could be long term consequences for the nation's spiritual and physical health. This is only one example of a challenge to traditional values which Christians face at 'the front line'.

Rachel Jenkins of the William Temple Foundation has written an 'Occasional Paper' to commemorate the lifelong work of Mark Gibbs who promoted the importance of lay people in the church and their influence in the world. A descriptive leaflet commending her paper says:

'For many people who once found a sense of vocation in their secular occupations, the radical changes of recent years in both public and private sectors have been dismaying. Yet the churches have rarely had the words or insights to offer more than platitudes.'

At the end of her paper, Rachel Jenkins writes this poem:[5]

'Sunday by Sunday
the church gathers
Women and men meet
to worship
to withdraw
from the world?
or to bring to the world
their living with them.

Women and men
living with tensions
struggling with dilemmas
challenged by change
oppressed by changes
that are too rapid.

Is this the place
is it together
that they can affirm
THIS is where life is
given meaning?

Or do they sing uneasily
because here is the place
where no meaning is given
to the context and the content
of their daily lives?

Can I bring my anger with me
Or must it be quelled before I enter?
Can I bring my confusion
Or should I simply pretend there is none?

What do I do with the contradictions
of loving my family

yet rarely seeing them?
or with the pressure to raise
excessive profits without
the tempering of justice
and compassion?

What do I do with the painful knowledge
of failing to touch with understanding
the urgent needs
of my fellow human beings?

Soothing will not ease my burdens.
Where do I find the courage
to confront my problems? . . .'

In this poem the lay person's cry is heard.

Ordained ministers should take that cry seriously and set aside time to listen carefully to the stories which lay people have to tell from the front line.

For it is only as ordained ministers hear the voice of those who work in the secular world at the front line, that an authentic connection can be made between Sunday and Monday.

It is only as the Church provides adequate opportunities for lay people to 'tell their story' that lay people can be encouraged with a gospel that is relevant to their need and be sustained for their ministry in the world.

CHAPTER THREE

Priorities for Ordained Ministry

Daily Tasks

Why is it that ordained ministers do not devote more time to the important task of empowering lay people? Why is the authentic lay person's cry so often not heard by the Church? How is it that so often the church on Sunday makes no connection with the world on Monday? How is it that the Church so often behaves like an inward-looking holy club? What are the distractions which cause the ordained ministers to divert their energy away from the task of supporting lay people in their 'front line' work in the secular world?

The reasons are many and various. It often amounts to a matter of priorities. There are so many things to be done within limited time. It is not my task to spell out all the reasons for this neglect in detail. That would be the task of the author of another book. It is certainly not because they are lazy! It is my experience that ordained ministers need no encouragement to work harder than they already do. They need encouragement to lead a more leisurely, more reflective style of life in the midst of the often hectic activity surrounding them. We should certainly not seek to make them feel 'guilty' about their lack of time to attend to these matters. It is

important to look at some of the tasks which engage the
energy of ordained ministers, for (important as they are) they
are often very time consuming.

They can be classified under a number of headings (not in
any order of priority):

> Prayer and Reading
> Public Worship and Evangelism
> The Congregation and the 'Parish'
> Administration
> Maintenance of Buildings
> Fund Raising
> Ministry to the Sick and to those who Suffer
> Ministry to Individuals/Individualism
> Theology
> Institutional Matters/Institutionalism

> and so on . . .

Prayer and Reading

I am not going to say much about prayer and reading in this
chapter. This is not because I think that it is of little or no
importance. On the contrary I think that it is of the greatest
importance. Every ordained minister's life must be under-
girded by prayer and reading. Time must be set aside for
reflection each day in order to relate biblical insights to
modern everyday living. I shall return to this topic in the
chapter on 'Spirituality for the Front Line'. Suffice it to say at
this point that I believe that it is almost as important for
ordained ministers to reflect in prayer upon the pages of a
newspaper as it is to reflect upon the pages of the Bible itself!
The prayers of ordained ministers should be informed by the
affairs of secular life in the world which God loves so much,
illuminated by the insights of the Gospel. Such prayer must be
a prelude to the task of equipping lay people for their ministry
in the world.

Worship and Evangelism

Similarly, of the many tasks undertaken by ordained ministers,
worship and evangelism are very high in the order of priorities.
Sadly, both worship and evangelism can sometimes cease to be

meaningful to congregations. This is apparent by the gradual decrease in church attendance.

There are many reasons for the decline in church attendance, but one reason is that those who attend say that the worship they participate in and the preaching which they hear does not match the daily experience of their work-a-day lives. This may be partly due to their minister's own lack of experience of ordinary people's lives, or (more generally) the preconceived aims and objectives of professional ordained ministers as they seek to satisfy the expectations of the institutional churches.

A simple remedy may be to create more opportunities for consultation between ordained ministers and lay people so that they may gain a better understanding of life at 'the front line'. There could also be value in a greater involvement of lay people in devising public worship and in assisting ordained ministers to prepare their sermons, following the example of Pastor Horst Symanoski in Germany.

The Congregation and the 'Parish'

The life of the congregation is very important, even among those churches which are not 'Congregationalist'. The Anglican Church, for example, seeks to take the 'Parish' very seriously. A parish is a particular geographical area with precise boundaries drawn on a map.

In theory the Anglican parish priest has a pastoral responsibility to all who reside in the parish whether they attend Church or not. The staffing of an Anglican parish actually depends, to a large extent, upon the number of people who reside within the parish boundaries. Thus a parish in which 25,000 people are employed within its boundaries but only 600 people reside there, may be regarded as a small or light duty parish, whereas a parish in which 25,000 people 'reside' but only 600 are employed within its boundaries by day is reckoned as a 'large parish' and the parish church may be staffed accordingly.

In practice however, the parish 'as such' is rarely, alas, taken seriously by the Church. The effective unit is the congregation. Ask the average Anglican clergymen to introduce you to his 'parishioners' on a Sunday and you will invariably meet the congregation! Members of the congregation are not concerned about boundaries on a map. People attend the church of their choice and will often travel many miles and across many parish boundaries to do so! In some parishes in Birmingham the majority of people in the parish are not Christian at all. They are of other faiths – Hindus and Muslims for example, whilst the local Christian congregation 'commutes' in (sometimes from a considerable distance) to attend 'their' parish church.

The subtle pressure upon Anglican clergy is therefore to create a 'gathered' church and build up the numbers in their congregation. Churches are of various traditions: high or low, evangelical or anglo-catholic, Book of Common Prayer or Alternative Service Book, etc. People worship according to their tradition, and where they feel 'comfortable'. In this process much depends upon the personality of the vicar!

So ordained ministers spend a lot of time preparing 'activities' of various kinds (often of a social nature) which take place in the church buildings and seek to maintain and extend the congregation.

Of course much of this work may be delegated to lay people, but if so, the danger is (unless it is undertaken by retired people or those who are not in full-time employment) that this may divert the energies of the best lay people from their effective lay ministry in their secular world!

Administration

An increasing amount of time and energy is spent by ordained ministers on administration. The larger the congregation becomes, so the greater is the need for efficient administration. Much of this can be delegated to lay people, but again in doing so some of the best lay people may be distracted from an effective ministry in their secular lives at the front line. On the other hand it is not always wise to delegate all the administration to retired people lest the leadership potential of younger people is neglected! This may be a 'Catch 22' situation.

Much of the paperwork comes in increasing quantity through the letter box from outside the parish: demands for statistics and reports of various kinds from church officials, registrars, city officials, etc. The daily post has to be dealt with, at least in part, by ordained ministers, hopefully with the help (but not always) of a secretary. Routine administration undertaken also includes preparing for meetings, talks, sermons etc. and making advance plans for the months ahead. Some matters have to be booked a year or more in advance! I have always maintained throughout my own ministry that a good secretary for the ordained minister is worth two assistants.

Computers and word processors are helpful but they are expensive and like the tide, they can create a momentum of their own. Administration can so easily divert attention away from the task of equipping lay people for effective lay ministry.

Maintenance of Buildings

This is a thorny problem! An Anglican parish may contain two people and a cow, but if it also contains an ancient parish church (which may not be pulled down), the priest in charge is frequently required to undertake a lot of maintenance work which can become an acute diversion from effective ministry. Buildings can be more demanding than people! Some vicars, however, revel in this, especially if the buildings are of architectural or historical importance. They may become devoted experts on the building and spend considerable time giving guided tours and public lectures on the fabric and monuments, etc!

Whether or not they see themselves as 'curators', the secular authorities frequently do so. In a recent survey undertaken by the Northampton civic authorities the curate of a Northampton Town Centre Church was actually described in the Report as the 'curator'! Was this a misprint or public perception?

Not all may wish to put the upkeep of ancient buildings high on their list of priorities. In Birmingham the Airport Chaplain is also priest-in-charge of a small hamlet parish in which the airport is situated. The appointment was made, so that in theory, the tiny hamlet parish would take up 25% of the incumbent's time leaving 75% of his time to an effective ministry to the airport. In practice, he finds that considerably more than 25% of his time is required by the parish . . . on maintaining the 'plant'!

This is in no way meant to diminish the importance of maintaining buildings, but simply to point out some of the difficulties that ordained ministers face as they seek to set their priorities. No doubt it was for this reason that several Anglican Dioceses have introduced 'Ministerial Development Interviews' (MDI) whereby senior clergy assist their colleagues to work out mutually agreed priorities and objectives for the year ahead. Like all such managerial techniques, there are dangers in MDI It is easy to measure success in numerical terms, but how can the success of supporting lay people in their front line secular tasks be quantified?

Fund Raising

Alongside maintaining buildings, the task of fund raising is another activity which not infrequently grips the attention of the ordained minister for many working hours. This is true whether we are talking in terms of 'beer and bingo' (popular 'Catholic' activities) or climbing steeples walking/running/cycling/swimming vast distances – a method of fund raising favoured by many deans and provosts!

Christian Stewardship is a preferred method, but the popular 'time, talents and money' approach seems to refer almost entirely to spare time activity for the church and 'disposable' income! Either way, ordained ministers can spend a lot of time diverting their lay people's attention away from their secular front line responsibilities.

Ministry to Sick and those who Suffer

Jesus spent a lot of time during his earthly life, ministering to the poor, healing the sick and enabling the people who experienced suffering to feel loved and wanted. He had a special concern for the outcast and those on the periphery of society.

It is important that the Church should minister to sick and suffering people. It is important that the Church should have a concern for those who are poor, homeless, unemployed and mentally ill, following the example of Jesus two thousand years ago. It is equally important to pay attention to the causes of sickness and disease and to those 'principalities' and 'powers' with responsibility for the distribution of wealth.

The clergy and congregation of Grace Cathedral in San Francisco USA engage in a special ministry to those who suffer from AIDS. At least two members of that Cathedral have died from AIDS, and it is very impressive to see the sensitive way in which members of the Cathedral congregation surround with love those who suffer. Nevertheless it does mean that the Cathedral is not undertaking ministry in other ways. There is very little attempt to minister to the 'principalities and powers' who run the City of San Francisco, very little attempt to 'influence the influencers'. No attempt is made to relate to business and professional people or to develop a relevant theology to support them in the daily decisions that have to be made.

'Given our priorities', said the Dean, 'there simply are not the resources for us to do this.'

David Logan, a businessman living near the Cathedral in San Francisco who also commutes regularly to London made the comment. 'Yes, but by caring for the poor, the Church can get shunted into a ghetto.'

In the United States of America the Church seems to give high priority to pastoral care and welfare work. On the other hand Industrial Mission and ministry to those who hold power (as opposed to those who are power-less) seems to have very low priority in the USA. The pioneering work of Scott Paradice in the motor industry in the 1970s seems to have collapsed. There are exceptions. A notable recent example of an effort to influence the 'principalities and powers' in the USA was the Roman Catholic Bishops' Pastoral Letter on Catholic Social Teaching and the US Economy entitled *Economic Justice For All*. This document made a big impact – comparable to the Anglican *Faith in the City* report.

Individualism

One of the reasons why ordained ministers are distracted from the task of ministering to those who are strong within secular institutions is that it is often easier to minister to those who are weak. These people have a more obvious need. Moreover the Church has a long tradition of ministering to individuals rather than to institutions and clergy are frequently not equipped for the latter more specialist task.

In spite of the emphasis, both in the Old Testament prophetic writings and in the teaching of Jesus, about the corporate nature of humanity and the importance of building a 'just society', the Church often finds it difficult to minister to corporate groups other than to individuals one by one within those groups. Individualism is very strong in America, and has been greatly encouraged in Britain during recent years. The American Sociologist, Professor Robert Bellah points out in his book *Habits of the Heart* that excessive individualism can be destructive to society. Religion is often regarded as something for the individual – private and personal. It is seen to be related to private and personal areas of life – the home, the family, recreation, etc. A great deal of writing has been done over the centuries on personal morality – matters of sexuality, marriage, personal relationships between individual people rather than between corporate groups, etc.

Comparatively little has been written on 'corporate ethics' and the conflicting values which arise in business and public institutions and in wider society.

Ministry to individual people is of great importance. Our Lord gave great attention to individuals as he also paid close attention to groups of people. Yet so long as clergy continue to emphasise personal and private aspects of life and concentrate their ministry on individuals within a private residential setting, the task of equipping lay people to exercise a ministry in their secular public 'front line', will have low priority.

Theology

There is a chapter in this book which deals with the subject of theology for the 'front line'. Theology is an important subject. The Christian theological understanding of humankind, for example, (as fallen yet potentially redeemable in Christ) provides a realistic assessment of human nature. Human beings are not totally corrupt. They do not need always to be treated with the carrot and the stick. But neither are they perfect, merely needing 'encouragement'. Christian theology is realistic about humankind. In industry many of the old 'time and motion' techniques, designed to obtain maximum productivity from a workforce proved to be unproductive in the long run owing to time lost because of disputes. In contrast some of the more productive and profitable companies are managed on a Christian assessment placing responsibility and trust upon people.

Institutionalism

Robert Bellah, in his book *The Good Society*, defines an institution as 'a patterned way which human beings have developed to live together'.

One of the reasons why the Church fails to empower lay people for a ministry in secular institutions is that the Church is itself an institution with paid officials and an organisational structure. The ecclesiastical world can be a world of its own. The secular world of lay ministry does not easily 'fit' into the institutional life of the Church and cannot easily be evaluated. Even non stipendiary priests in the Anglican Church do not easily 'fit' into Anglican organisational structures.

Many of the most able clergy are completely absorbed into the institutional life of the Church. They spend many hours sitting on numerous committees entirely devoted to ecclesiastical matters which make very little impact upon the world which God loves so much.

Fortunately Christians believe in transformation by the power of Christ. Christ not only transforms the lives of individual people but he also transforms the lives of institutions.

The Church is an Institution.
The Church can be transformed!
That is our ground for hope!

In this chapter we have discussed some of the reasons why ordained ministers sometimes fail to provide an effective support to lay people at the front line in secular life. Clergy are frequently too pre-occupied with other tasks from which, ideally, they should be freed! Faced with a multiplicity of jobs it is not always easy to see which are the more important. Fortunately, many ordained ministers realise this and make use of 'job counsellors' to assist them and prioritise. High on the list of priorities should be the task of encouraging lay people to 'tell their story'.

CHAPTER FOUR

Stories from the Front Line

'My vicar is so busy that he hasn't got the time to listen to my story, so I won't burden him with it.'

This cry from the heart reflects the sad fact that ordained ministers are often so bogged down with the kind of ecclesiastical activities described in the previous chapter that they have no time to listen to the stories that lay people want to tell about their experiences at the front line.

This chapter records a few typical stories about people in secular occupations. These stories have been collected in a number of different ways. Some people wrote them down. Others told their stories during public worship or through an informal conversation. A variety of men and women tell their story in this chapter. They are all true. The story tellers include a Chief Executive of a major city, a politician, an accountant, and those who work in commerce, industry and the professions.

The Front Line in a Major City

The first story has been written by the Chief Executive of a major city in the West Midlands.

'My everyday life working in a political democracy is involved with trying to serve the wishes of my political masters, reconciling and prioritising needs in our community and trying to achieve my own goals for management within a large complex organisation. That's hard, but doing it in a way which adheres to Christian principles adds a dimension. Take a few examples:

If you work for a Council that supports policies inconsistent with your religious beliefs and you are caught up in administering these policies, what should you do? People have in the past found difficulty with policies as far apart as Sunday trading, birth control and religious tolerance. Should there be an opportunity for a conscience "get out" and a "no victimisation" agreement if you really and sincerely do not believe it right to pursue a certain line? Or does adhering to the employer's policies go with the implied threat "put up with it or get out"? We quickly get into a complex of deeply difficult concerns about the extent of an employer's (and employee's) rights. Can the employer insist on certain things? Should the employee be prepared to resign?

A second area concerns the consideration one applies to the issues coming before you. Is the employee entitled in the absence (as will usually be the case) of explicit guidance – to prioritise or adjust his response to third parties having regard to the principles of his or her faith, and so relegate to the bottom of the in-tray those organisations whose actions or beliefs offend his or her principles? A firm trading with South Africa might have been an example or an organisation guilty of racial discrimination.

The mirror side of that issue concerns the employee in a pro-active stance: is it right for him to concentrate his own initiatives in areas supporting his own faith or beliefs – for example an Inner City Partnership skewed in the direction of one faith or denomination – and provide an easier track for people of his own persuasion to get into his diary?

Lastly the issue of how you comport yourself. Do you treat your staff and colleagues in a way which is consistent with your beliefs? Is it possible to resist the temptation to gossip, scheme behind people's backs, use bad language, not accord others their dignity?

The footnote is a reminder that the most difficult problem is not resolving these difficulties, but remembering that they exist. Having a faith at work means not forgetting what you believe on Sunday! A bit more understanding help in some of these quite impossible dilemmas would be gratefully received!'

The Front Line in a Multi-National Company

The next story comes from a senior executive in a large multi-national company. What is special about this story is that the senior executive who tells the story is also a priest. He is a non stipendiary minister. He told his story to a congregation during evening worship.

'I am not an Industrial Chaplain. I am not paid by the Church. I am not paid to be a priest. I am paid by my company to work for them. I am not paid to be a pseudo-vicar. I have been ordained for just over three years and I still have not taken a wedding, a baptism or a funeral! I am not even paid to solve pastoral problems. I am paid to be an engineer.

I got a first class degree in engineering. I am good at my job. So when I told my boss I wanted to be ordained and that I still wanted to continue to work for the company as an engineer he said to me, "Can you do that?" He expected me to leave the company and go into the "Church"[sic].

But I belong in industry. It is my vocation to work in industry. To leave industry to go into the Church would be to say that there is either something very wrong with industry or something very wrong with the Church.

Some people may think that being a priest in industry is an impossible combination. I work in the process industry, with all the day-to-day problems of pollution and environmental issues. For many years I was involved in the manufacture of carbon fibres for aerospace and military purposes. We even helped to create a personal anti-tank missile! Being involved in that sort of thing and being a priest seems to startle some people. They say, You can't do that!

I've had experience as a purchasing manager. This means screwing the best deal out of people. I am good at that. But some people say to me, "As a priest, you can't do that!"

I say to them. "That's tough. God can". That's where I happen to be. I am in industry. I am committed to industry. And I am a priest. Is that an impossible vocation? Maybe. Yet ministry is involvement in impossibilities. I am a minister in secular employment.

The situation where I am involves tensions, ambiguities and compromises. But these are no different from those of any Christian in the secular world. Being a priest makes the Church take more notice of the tensions that we all live in.

We cannot do that! But God can, in each one of us. We are all, as Christians, rooted in the world and at the same time rooted in the Church. That is what incarnation is all about. Jesus of Nazareth lived His life in the secular world. As Christians we are called to work for justice and mutual care in the world. Industry exists for the benefit of all people. It's a hard slog. There are budgets and deadlines. Yet, management is a caring profession and when I see a caring manager I see God at work. My task is to point to signs of God's Kingdom.

So we are concerned about environmental improvement. This says something about the theology of co-creation. We are concerned with improving standards of safety in the chemical industry. This says something about penitence. We are concerned about creating an environment where people can learn to trust one another and talk to each other about those things that go wrong. This says something about faith.

One day, because of the recession, we had to close our department. Despite all the pain and the trauma, we were able to close that department in a caring way. The management were thanked for the caring way in which it was done. That's a sign of the Kingdom.

One of the new methods being promoted in modern industry is called Total Quality. All Christians should be in the front line – where the action is – promoting new ways of working, improving the quality of life at work and seeking better quality and reliability in our products – being there and pointing to signs of God's presence. Doing the impossible. That is what we should be doing – rather than busying ourselves in our churches.'

An Accountant's Story

I have listened to several accountants telling their story. Their profession is full of pitfalls and temptations. One accountant described his life as like 'working in a jungle'. He implied that people often tried to bribe him to distort the truth. This particular accountant was looking forward to his retirement and seemed afraid to tell his story.

But another accountant sent me this true story. It is a long and complicated story that illustrates some of the ghastly things that may go wrong, he writes:

'In the late summer of 1988 I was introduced to the overseas general manager of a very successful company who was seeking to raise a quarter of a million pounds to enable him to buy back his company from the present owners.

He had pioneered and patented a new building system in the early 1960s which was used throughout the Third World through his own company. As the company needed further capital he had agreed to sell out to his present employers who were now using his experience in running large overseas building contracts and under-utilising the opportunities for his building system.

It was now his wish to return to the UK for family and health reasons and follow up the firm enquiries that were being received.

He indicated that he and three associates had raised £130,000 through a holding company which would own sixty per cent of the new company and that he sought an additional £120,000 and bank support from the other investors.

I became a substantial minority investor in the new consortium and arranged banking facilities so that the buyout was able to proceed in September of that year. I became Financial Director and represented the minority shareholders on the parent board. The chief shareholder, initially would be spending most of his time abroad developing his extensive business contacts for the benefit of the company before taking up residence in the UK in the following year.

In the first two months of operation many expensive overseas trips were undertaken following up firm enquiries for the building system. After protracted negotiations the establishment of a joint venture was agreed to develop a new office and hotel complex in central Russia.

As one million pounds was needed, the financial implications for us were larger than we could manage. So we sought a further major investor. We opened successful conversations with a leading finance house inviting them to join us in a venture with considerable long term benefits. They put up the finance for the entry into the Russian market and took two thirds of the equity in a new joint venture company.

Several expensive trips to Russia led to a need for a larger overdraft for our company to see the joint venture through. The bankers agreed on the promise of personal guarantees from me and the other key directors and shareholders. Facilities of £80,000 were agreed on the strength of the Russian contract and, as Financial Director, I signed a personal guarantee with the assurance that my key colleagues would sign on their return from Russia.

Events then moved swiftly. Two major investors in the parent company complained to me that they had not received share certificates for their investment. On investigation I could find no trace of this money having been invested in the company. It became obvious that, as it had been paid to the chief shareholder, he had used the money for other purposes. Further investigations led us to discover that he was an undischarged bankrupt.

I was now in a dilemma. The need for our colleague to be overseas was just a "front" to deceive us and I was personally guaranteeing the bank overdraft alone approaching a sum of £80,000. Confidence with the bank would be shattered if I told them the true situation. Moreover the other directors would probably avoid signing the guarantee. We would also be in danger of being taken over by the bank when we could not fulfil our part of the contract.

There was an even stronger call and that was one's own professional integrity as a Christian. My fellow shareholders had been defrauded and we were in the control of a dishonest man who had deceived us. Even worse, it transpired that the Chairman had known that our chief shareholder was a bankrupt but had failed to disclose it.

On the chief shareholder's return I decided to confront him and all the shareholders with the truth. I insisted that he immediately sign the guarantee and pay the monies due to the company from the other shareholders he had misappropriated. This he refused to do. His argument was that he was owed the money for goodwill for his patents, and that by unmasking him I would be destroying everyone's investment and the huge potential for gain to all of the shareholders by the Russian joint venture.

Two days later, whilst considering my position, I was

removed as Financial Director by a shareholders' majority resolution. This meant loss of control over my minority invest-ment, telling the bank the reasons for my removal which led to the call up of my personal guarantee.

Standing up for truth I lost my job, a good salary and a potentially successful future. I faced many worrying weeks before alternative bankers were found and the bank guarantee removed. My investment in the company remains locked in.'

The author of this story added these words in a personal letter which he wrote to me:

'This is a true story which shows that standing up for truth can be very costly. It was for me – but there is value in being at peace with God and yourself.'

The Front Line in a Board Room written by a Company Chairman

This short story is an extract from a letter written to me by a successful businessman (but modest about his success) who is also a very prominent Methodist lay person. He wrote this letter to me in response to my request for his 'story'. It demonstrates that some lay people do get the support they need!

'For myself, I can only say that the Church has given me all the support I could wish for. It has taught me such tech-niques as I know about running a business, analysing situations and illustrating life. Not that I would claim to be "much cop" as a businessman – I just run a slightly expanded shop at a corner and that not particularly well at this moment.

It was you who made an unforgettable remark when you said to me that the advantage of being an industrial chaplain was that it gave you an entrée into the business part of the world, and that YOU could listen and learn.

For myself, I cannot run a business without the support I receive from the Church and I cannot worship without bringing my part of the world through the door.

Yes, I have to admit, most people leave their part of the world in the porch, in a sort of spiritual umbrella stand, before they go into church. Well, the leaders of worship could go and tell them to bring it in!'

The Front Line in Industrial Relations

The next story has been written by a former senior executive in the engineering industry who became well known in the West Midlands Engineering Employers' Association at a time when the industrial relations scene in the West Midlands was passing though a particularly difficult period.'

He writes:

'It was a cold November morning in Cambridge when I bicycled up to the lower end of Portugal Place with my mind more on my uncertain future than on where I was steering. My dilemma was a choice between offering myself for ordination or going to Birmingham to do an industrial relations job. By some strange coincidence the person into whom I had bicycled was my vicar. I shared my doubts about the direction of my vocation and he, nursing a bruised leg, encouraged me to keep faith with Christ as I took one step at a time. This helped, but never quite removed, the tension in my mind about the high value of ordination and the low value of business.

I chose the low road and went to Birmingham, a place in which "swarms of people made things under a cloud of soot" according to my great aunt. From the moment I arrived in my first job I remained uncertain about the value of my work as a vocation in God's eyes. This must have shown because I was told that unless I sorted this out I would be sacked. At this stage I met another vicar who had been confronted with some middle aged businessmen wrestling with the same tensions that were testing me. They had just become Christians as a result of attending one of Billy Graham's meetings at Haringey in 1957. We shared the same question, "How was it possible to be a Christian in business?"

The vicar challenged us to make a connection between the first chapter of St Paul's letter to the Colossians and the process of business. We discovered a different sort of Christ who held people, money and material together regardless of our success or failure. We were able to make a link between this Christ's function in reconciling these things and our function in managing towards a balance and direction. He gave me a new insight into my job as a calling and saved me from the sack!

I found that this understanding of Christ's work in the

process of business gave me a deeper and more radical insight into the dynamics of a business situation. It made prayer and management a more creative experience as a "whole". To my surprise it increased my cutting edge in business rather than blunting my ability. By this I do not mean that I became more ruthless but I was able to handle a business situation without the need to defend myself. For example, I found that by admitting error, all those involved became more constructive towards a reconciliation.

Now, some thirty five years after that chance meeting in Cambridge, it is my turn to be a middle aged businessman. Most of us involved in those early days met recently for a reunion. Without exception our grey hairs revealed the wounds of business life. Some of us had experienced the pain of drawing the short straw in the turmoil of mergers, others had reached the plateau of their career and were leading dissatisfied lives waiting for their pensions and one had given his all to his business and, in doing so, had lost his wife. For me these experiences had more to do with bereavement than with failure. I think I can now understand the sense of pain that Christ must feel as He holds together the process of business and suffers as each vested interest refuses reconciliation but is unable to win. How can I interpret the Cross to those interests so that the purpose of Christ becomes the purpose of business?'

A Christian at the Front Line in Politics

I invited a well known politician, who had spent over twenty five years on the front benches (both in government and opposition) to give a Lent Address about his 'front bench' experience as a Christian. This distinguished politician happens to be a member of my church and he is a member of the Parochial Church Council! Little did I know, when I invited him, that he would be giving his address a few days after the announcement of the date of the 1992 election! He himself, was not seeking re-election. Nonetheless, this was risky and I waited in some trepidation to receive 'flak' from those who were not of his political persuasion. I had not planned to invite representatives of other political parties to mount the pulpit during Lent!

This is a summary of what he said on that occasion:

'Politics is about the art and the science of government. What concerns us as Christians is the true purpose of government and how we achieve that purpose.

I believe that God's will on earth (our daily prayer) is the true purpose of politics. That means establishing the ethics of Christ. In numerous passages in the Bible, we find that politics walks hand in hand with Christianity.

In an early chapter of Genesis we read how Cain murdered his brother Abel because of his jealousy. When challenged by God, Cain replied, "Am I my brother's keeper?" No Christian can escape from that challenge. All of us have the responsibility of "keeping" our brothers and sisters. Politics is the means we have to achieve this end. Jesus knew this. That is why he taught that we must render unto Caesar the things that are Caesar's and unto God the things that are God's. The context of this teaching is important. The Pharisees had come to Jesus with a trap question suggesting that there was a conflict between duty to the State and duty to God. Jesus called the Pharisees "hypocrites"! Duty to God and duty to the State are two sides of the same coin. That is why we are to love God and love our neighbours as ourselves. All political questions have ethical dimensions. To be our brother's keeper and to love our neighbour as ourselves is the true purpose of politics and provides a daunting challenge.

The ways to achieve this may vary according to the political party we choose. In a democracy collective wisdom is considered to be important. Silence or neutrality is not an option for Christians in politics. As Edmond Bourke once said, "All that is necessary for the triumph of evil is for good men to remain silent." '

Having outlined his Christian philosophy, the Member described his 37 years experience in Parliament which included over 25 years on the front benches both in government and opposition. He illustrated the twin need for both political and ethical judgement with a number of examples.

'In 1955 Britain declared war on Egypt in defiance of the advice of the United Nations and many of her allies, following Nasser's seizure of the Suez Canal.

The ensuing turmoil provided cover for Russia to invade Hungary and Czechoslovakia. The nation was divided over this matter. So was Parliament. On one day the Speaker had to suspend sittings on two occasions. In the end, the moral force of the United Nations prevailed, but it took another forty years before Hungary regained her freedom.

Today we face new dilemmas following the collapse of Communism in Eastern Europe. How should the free world respond? Should we unhesitatingly use our surplus food supplies to feed the hungry or should we take a longer term view? We must pray that governments take the right decisions. Our commitment to God allows us no prevarication. In my judgement we failed Gorbachev. We must not fail Yeltsin, for if we do fail him Russia may return to totalitarianism. That is a major political and moral dilemma for us all.

As Minister for Sport I was faced with the terrible problem of apartheid. At that time the South African Government refused to allow the English Selectors to choose Basil d'Olivera for an English touring side in South Africa. I could not tolerate that! Let us pray that the new hope for future South Africa in 1992 may not be crushed at birth. The d'Olivera experience taught me that for a Christian there is no hiding place. Our arguments must proceed from our convictions.

National political life is full of issues which have a moral as well as a technical dimension. Policies must be judged on whether they do or do not promote the interests of us all . . . our neighbours as well as ourselves.

In my constituency in Small Heath in Birmingham's inner city, we have an unemployment rate of over 33%. Over 50% of our young people leaving school cannot find jobs. We also have the highest numbers of one parent families to be found in this city and we have the highest rate of infant mortality (22 deaths for every 1,000 live births) in Europe. We have one of the highest ethnic populations of any constituency in Britain. We have social problems of every type. There is a widespread feeling among many people that they are "trapped". For a few, their problems are of their own making. But most people are genuine victims of bureaucracy or are overwhelmed by circumstances. They demand our care and our compassion, for we ARE our "brother's keeper". For me, that is what Christianity is all about when we pray "Thy Will be done on earth as it is in Heaven".'

The politician quoted the hymn written by Frank Mason North:

'Where cross the crowded ways of life
Where sound the cries of race and clan
Above the noise of selfish strife
We hear thy voice O Son of Man.'

And then continued:

'Our faith tells us that so much of the social life of this country and so many of the evils of the world are contrary to the Christian faith. St James in the second chapter of his Epistle reminds us that faith without action is a barren philosophy. Christian conscience and concern has to express itself as a positive and caring force. Politics is a means of caring, righting wrong, and doing something about it. Jesus says: "Inasmuch as ye have done it unto one of the least of these my brethren, ye have done it unto me." ' [Matthew 26 v 40]

The Member ended his address by quoting from a Persian Christian, Karlil Gibran:

'Is not religion all deeds and all reflection
Who can separate his faith from his actions?
Or his belief from his occupations?
Your daily life is your temple and your religion.
Whenever you enter into it, take with you your ALL.'

The Front Line as Chief Executive of a Federation

This story is part of an interview with the Chief Executive of a Federation. He began by describing a typical day:

'I arrive at the office at 8.30am after a difficult one hour drive from my home. If I am ten minutes late in leaving I can be held up in terrible traffic jams. On the way to the office I listen to the radio, sometimes Radio 3 and sometimes "Thought for the Day". I listen to the radio with half my brain. The other half of my brain is getting ready for the day's work.

When I arrive at the office I go round saying "hello" to people. I think that's important and it is appreciated. Then I sit down and start dealing with the post, preparing agendas for the day's meetings and reading the results of meetings that have taken place during the previous week. The phone calls begin early! There are numerous phone calls throughout the day. Each day is different. It is impossible to predict what will happen.

A day which is all "my day" (a day which I can completely control) is very rare. The phone brings problems which need my attention. That can induce stress, for if I spend much of the day on the telephone, it means that "my own work" may have to be left to the end of the day. I often stay late at the office to get the work finished. I do not like taking work home. Fortunately I have a good secretary (I prefer to call her my personal assistant), and I am learning more and more the importance of delegation. I do not find it easy to delegate. I am a perfectionist but I am continually surprised by the intelligence, initiative and trustworthiness of people around me. I say "I would like you to do that", and the reply comes back "I have already done it". I find that the task has been done to a very high standard. That increases my confidence. I know that I CAN delegate without worrying. It is a matter of putting trust in my staff and giving them the opportunity to demonstrate how good they are. If I do everything myself it is not good for them and it is not good for me!

In addition to the daily pressures there are the difficulties I have in holding together a large Federation. Each association is important and wants to "stand on its own feet" and to go its own way! I find a tendency for each association to raise its own profile and therefore the profile of the Federation is suppressed. The dilemma I have is how far I fight to maintain the high profile of the Federation at the expense of the profile of each individual association. For me that is a moral dilemma. It means that I sometimes have to swallow my pride as Chief Executive of the Federation. I have to say to myself that the Chief Executive is not important. It is the companies that join the Federation who are important. They need support, particularly in times of recession when so many companies are vulnerable and can "go to the wall". Member companies need our help and guidance and they look to their association for that support.

I find that I can think about God during my day at work. That does not always solve my problems, but very often it does! I find that a "small voice" from within speaks to me. Let me give some examples:

I can think of one person who used to irritate me. He

generated an atmosphere of conflict and I responded in like manner. But the "voice inside me" said "This is not the way to handle this situation. Turn the other cheek." I did so and by golly it worked! Suddenly I did not allow that person's attitude to annoy me. I introduced a lighter conversation. It changed our whole relationship.

I can think of somebody who did not give sufficient time to the department for which he had responsibility. The members of that department became frustrated. But, once again that "voice within" spoke. It dawned on me that he had his own problems which sapped his time and energy and he felt embarrassed about it. So he became aggressive. This was his defence mechanism. When I became aware of this we responded differently. He realised that he need no longer be defensive. He need not try to impress us! He could rely upon us.

Soon after I was appointed Chief Executive I discovered that we had obtained blanket cover not to employ people with disabilities of any kind on the grounds of inadequate ground floor toilet facilities and too many stairs. I was appalled. For example I knew that, whilst we may not be able to employ people without legs we could easily employ partially sighted people or those with hearing difficulties! So I arranged for a lady with impaired hearing to join the staff. Because of her deafness there were problems with this appointment, but our staff rallied round and supported her. When things got very difficult, a deputation came to me and said, "You are not going to sack her, are you?!" Fortunately, we were able to move her to another department. My decision has been justified and she has gained a lot of confidence. People matter. It is possible to spend all day worrying about finances and you can easily forget about people who need a helping hand. I believe in love. I do not like to see people treated badly.

These are just a few examples of the ways in which my faith helps me whilst I work in my office. My faith also helps me as I drive home at the end of the working day, when I reflect upon all that has happened including the things that cause stress and strain. I am enabled to see things in perspective. For me, spirituality does not mean thinking hard about God. Spirituality simply means bringing God into my thinking.

Sometimes I say "God, that was a hell of a day, wasn't it?", I believe that God understands. God has a sense of humour!'

The Front Line in the Newspaper Industry

'I work in the marketing side of newspapers. I am not directly responsible for what ends up in print in the same way that a journalist writes his news story. Yet there is a strong sense that we all contribute towards the product. We all share the praise and the blame.

The relationship between a newspaper and its readers is very close. The paper is invited into the household, often as a "friend". It sets standards. The newspaper industry is highly visible and commercially driven. Yet it may be more sensitive than other industries about its "commercialism". This can give rise to dishonesty when price rises become necessary. A newspaper, in common with other businesses, may portray itself as the reluctant passer on of increased costs when it might be more honest to say that it had increased the price by as much as it could get away with!

There are several moral aspects which concern me as a Christian. I am uneasy about the inclusion of horoscopes. If I were to suggest that horoscopes may not be ethically desirable, I would be confronted with the argument that if it is what people want, then give it to them! The overriding criteria in deciding whether something should or should not be included in a newspaper seems to be "Will it attract more readers than it puts off?"

This is, to some extent, ameliorated by the fact that, from an advertiser's point of view, there are desirable readers (with money) and undesirable readers (without money)! On this basis the "quality" newspapers are able to survive without horoscopes. But should such decisions be left purely to the whims of the market place? Do we give people what they want or do we give them what we think they need or what is good for them? I think that it is as wrong for a newspaper to lose its view of what is right and what is wrong (and simply tell people what they want to hear) as it would be for a church to do so.

Other moral dilemmas concern advertising. How far should advertisements merely give information and how far should they become manipulative? Where do we draw the line? What about honesty?

There are also certain values inherent in the actual content of news stories. How many positive lead stories can be found compared with stories concerned with scandal and pre-occupation with sex? It is said that bad news sells newspapers. Good news does not.

Much depends upon the responsibility of the readers. My advice to readers would be "read critically and read actively". As an employee of a newspaper I have very little power. The real power lies with the readers of the newspaper. If fifty Christians write to the editor about a matter which concerns them, their voice will be heard!'

Front Line Stories in Family Life

The family is an important institution which in many subtle ways has been transformed in recent years. I invited one of the central Presidents of the Mothers' Union to speak about the changing patterns of family life in Britain today. This is what she said:

'What sort of picture do you conjure up in your mind when you think of a family? There are so many varieties. Perhaps you think of the nuclear family: mother, father and two children. Some may call to mind the large and extended Victorian family. There are single parent families or families where two or more friends share a house. The word "family" can mean different things to different people.

Nowadays many families are living in very difficult circumstances. There are more homeless people, more people living alone and far more single parents with their children than there were thirty years ago. Whether unmarried, separated or divorced, the quality of life is different when children live with one parent instead of having two parents to care for them. The tensions and responsibilities for that parent are much greater. Children of one parent families often have more difficulty in relating to partners when they grow up. Seventy per cent of single parents are on income support in Britain. This means that they are having to "exist" from week to week or even day to day.

Loneliness is another problem. Human beings need someone to talk to. For this reason single parents often seek casual partners. Mum gets a boyfriend and further difficulties begin. Baby sitters are brought in. The boyfriend resents the time that Mum spends with the children. This may even lead to physical abuse of the children. Most physical and sexual child abuse is perpetrated by step-parents.

One of the prime reasons for homelessness among young people is because mother has a boyfriend and they are pushed out of their home or they leave because they are unhappy there. Homeless teenage girls often feel that they can improve their situation by becoming pregnant. They need someone to love and they need to be loved. Once they have had a baby they can get accommodation but only then do they realise their responsibilities for a little human being who cries and demands attention. These teenage girls have very few resources to cope with their responsibilities.

Often the accommodation that teenage mothers are given is not suitable. They may have to live in a high rise flat with a lift that is out of order because of vandalism. They are lonely and feel vulnerable. What they really need is private accommodation with communal rooms where they can cook meals with others in a similar situation. In the Birmingham Bull Ring Centre teenage girls with their babies can often be seen sitting huddled together for warmth and companionship. Their children are ill-fed and ill-clad.

There are other problems. Stories are told about elderly people living lonely and isolated lives in flats with water running down the walls. The isolation is made worse by poor public transport. In one hamlet in the Polesworth area (once a thriving mining community) there is only one bus per week to Tamworth and that is the only day when the elderly people can do their shopping.

Unemployment brings further hardship to families especially those with large mortgages. It is not unusual for the family house to be repossessed.

There are also the pressures which children have to face from their peers. The pressure put upon them to wear the "right" clothes (for example, expensive "trainers") is quite severe. Children are frequently bullied by their peers if their parents cannot afford these items. They are bombarded by the advertisements in the media so that they feel that they ought to have these things.

Families need support to cope with these problems. They need opportunities to express their anger and frustrations safely.

They need help in order to be able to VALUE themselves. They need time for people to listen to them. Victorian times were hard but at least there were members of the family in the same street and good friends just down the road. Times have changed. One in three marriages now ends in separation or divorce.

The Church has an important role in encouraging "bridge-building". We need to care for young people and take time to understand them. Christians should keep themselves informed about problems and issues. We should not be judgemental. The Church is commissioned with a Gospel of Good News for the poor. Poverty is rife in Britain today and action speaks louder than words.'

Sunday Trading

I conclude this chapter on 'Stories from the Front Line' with a story of a different kind – the ongoing saga of Sunday Trading.

This contribution to the debate has been written by a Christian who, until recently held a key position within the Consumers' Association.

' "Consumers" organisations have long supported the removal of restrictions on shop-opening hours – not just on Sundays – believing that shops should be open when people want to buy, not when sellers want to sell. This is the situation already in Scotland without apparently disastrous results. Consumers are sensitive to the needs of workers, they are usually workers themselves, but they believe that employment legislation should be sufficiently strong and enforceable to prevent exploitation. The present situation where the legislation is noticeably not enforced in many areas, brings all the law into disrepute while we await judgement* from the European Court and Government action.

Certainly protection of workers is a strong argument. Yet already many people work for our benefit on Sundays, not only in the police, fire brigade, hospitals and other caring professions, but in many factories, if need arises. Sundays today are more like weekly Bank Holidays than they are like Victorian Sundays. As the family climbs into the car, fills up

---

*We have now received a judgement from the European Court which gives each nation the right to take unilateral action.

with petrol at the petrol-station, which in many areas has taken the place of the village shop, it usually heads off to a place of leisure, sport or entertainment. Hundreds of people are employed at football and cricket grounds, racing circuits, pubs, stately homes, cinemas or driving coaches, in television and radio, as security guards. Are we happy about their conditions of employment? How many of us took an active and informed interest in recent discussions at European level about the 48 hour week?

There are those who now favour some compromise by which certain trading activities might be allowed – garden centres, DIY stores, the smaller cornershop (often opening very early and still open very late). These are convenient for the "culture of contentment". They won't cause disruption to the car-washing, pub-going and other entertainments of the average middle-class Sunday, while giving the imprimatur to home decorating and gardening. They are mostly irrelevant to the unemployed urban poor except as possible sources of employment.

How do we as Christians make a judgement? We certainly need to protect a day of rest, but we have to accept that for most people that is not attending church or sitting idly at home. We need to ensure that people should be free to worship and we should seek to establish an enforceable employment conscience clause for all faiths for all days of the week. Those who continue to oppose trading in shops in contrast to trading in entertainments need to be clear what the difference is. We need to establish that liberalising shop-opening hours is not the same as forcing shops to open when customers want them shut. We need to ensure that our Sunday worship is something special for us, to make it welcoming for others and to show a positive not a negative face to the world.'[1]

These are typical stories from the 'front line'. They illustrate the great variety of tensions and conflicts which people face in their day-to-day lives. I shall be commenting upon them and the issues which they raise during the course of this book.

> Stories are important.
> They need to be told!
> We need to LISTEN!

CHAPTER FIVE

Reactions from Command Headquarters

Stories from the 'front line' can be received with mixed reactions back at command headquarters. Responses can range from 'Do nothing' to 'My God, something must be done immediately!' Bishops and other Church leaders (like Generals) might not always hear the correct message or they may be tempted to take panic measures. A well known (apocryphal?) story tells how the signal dispatched from the front line as 'Rommel's captured send reinforcements' ended up at CommandHQ as 'Camel's ruptured send three and fourpence'. The story illustrates how easily wrong interpretations can be placed upon cries for help!

Hopefully it is now recognised at 'command headquarters' of the Church Militant here on earth that more effective structures should be devised to support lay people in their front line ministry. How best can they be established? The 'knee jerk' reaction to do something quickly without careful thought must be resisted. As the marriage service declares in the Book of Common Prayer, 'this is not by any to be enterprised, nor taken in hand, unadvisedly, lightly, or wantonly; but reverently, discreetly, soberly, and in the fear of God . . .!'

There are many pitfalls! The temptation may exist to set

up structures to support lay people in the 'front line' of public life without reference to structures that already exist. There are also dangers of tokenism. There is the temptation for ordained ministers to take initiatives without paying sufficient attention to the difficult secular issues which confront lay people, so that the so-called 'training' and 'education' devised by ordained ministers sometimes bears little or no relationship to the actual situations in which lay people find themselves. It is important that initiatives to support lay people in secular institutions should not be clerically dominated.

In many of the best support structures that already exist, lay people themselves have taken the initiative. In Great Britain, the Christian Association of Business Executives and the Institute of Business Ethics are national LAY-led initiatives offering support to business executives as they make decisions at the 'front line' in commerce and industry.

The same is true of initiatives in the United States of America such as the San Francisco Bay Area Ethics Consortium and the Vesper Society. In both these organisations the responsibility for leadership is with lay people.

There is a lot of experience in the support groups which have already been established for Lay People in Public life in how to deal with both 'individual' and 'corporate' ethics. It is important that the experience already gained should be collated in order that well-intentioned ordained ministers do not 're-invent the wheel'!

A recent initiative taken at Westhill College in Birmingham is attempting to collate this knowledge.

The Westhill College Initiative: Christians in Public Life Programme

A consultation was held in September 1991 at Westhill College Birmingham to consider support systems for Christians in Public Life in Britain and is in the process of establishing a comprehensive network. (See p. 182 for Summary of Report.)

By 'Public Life' is meant the major institutions of the CORPORATE life of society – social, educational, economic, commercial, political, etc.

In using the word 'institutions' in this book, I am following the definition offered by Bellah who defines institutions as 'the patterned ways which human beings have developed in order to live together'.[1]

Bellah points out how institutions have a very powerful influence over those people who operate within them often shaping attitudes and opinions.

Fifty-seven people attended the consultation at Westhill College, representing a wide cross-section of organisations which already seek to offer support to lay people in the 'front line'. Delegates included Industrial Chaplains, members of the Industry Churches' Forum (formerly the Industrial Christian Fellowship), sector and non stipendiary ministers, people in adult education and religious orders.

I am grateful to David Clark of Westhill College for drawing my attention to the following points which were raised at that consultation:

The Westhill Consultation identified the failure of the Church to equip lay people for their ministry and mission in public life. It noted the Church's continuing retreat from the 'public' into the 'private' sphere of life and the Church's reluctance to engage with new situations and new challenges.

Certain 'signs of hope and new beginnings' were, however, highlighted at the Consultation including the work of Industrial Mission in engaging with secular economic life; the initiatives of William Temple College (now in Manchester); the Luton Industrial Mission and various national initiatives such as the Anglican *Faith in the City* Report and the Methodist *Ministry of the People of God in the World*.

However the conference report added these ominous words:

'Despite these initiatives however, the ministry of the vast majority of Christians in public life remains unaffirmed, unsupported and often unknown.'

Features of Christian Mission and Ministry in Public Life

The briefing paper prepared for the Westhill Consultation stated that: 'The nature of Christian mission and ministry in public life is no easier to define than the diversity of Christian mission and ministry in general. However, the fact that Christian mission in public life has to take public life seriously (and cannot engage with it otherwise) highlights certain key missionary principles. The world's agenda has to be addressed with considerable respect, care and expertise.'

The briefing paper reminded delegates that at the conclusion of St Matthew's Gospel we are told how the risen Jesus goes on ahead of the disciples into Galilee, the place where Jesus conducted his public ministry. Our risen Lord Jesus STILL goes on ahead of us into 'Galilee' . . . the place of public ministry where we can discover Him. The modern Galilee may be Barclays Bank plc or the local Social Security office. Christ goes on ahead of us into these places.

Christians encounter and discover Christ already at work within secular institutions. Our task is to discover what Christ would have us do there and be His witnesses within those institutions.

Addressing the Task

The briefing paper prepared for the delegates who attended the initial Consultation at Westhill College makes a number of helpful suggestions:

1. The Churches must AFFIRM the ministry of lay people at the 'front line'.

2. The Churches should encourage and enable Christians to engage in informative 'social analysis' of secular society and the role of the church within 'secular society'.

3. The Churches should assist Christians to develop a theology and missiology for ministry within society.

4. The Churches should establish communities of faith in addition to local 'residentially' based congregations. (Some organisations, such as Industrial Mission are attempting to do this already.)

5. The Churches should encourage appropriate forms of spirituality for lay people who work in the public sphere and attempt to make the normal liturgical life of the church more relevant to secular public life.

6. The Churches should develop ways in which Christians in public life can be given adequate pastoral support – including forms of self-appraisal and personal guidance.

A New Role for the Ordained Ministry

David Clark in his consultation 'Briefing Paper' points out that all this will involve a new role for the ordained ministry. Industrial Mission and certain other specialised ministries have for many years pioneered the roles of catalyst, facilitator and theological consultant.

The new role for ordained ministers should encompass the need to:

1. Identify and affirm Christians in their public domain.

2. Assist Christians to engage in social analysis, theological reflection and the formulation of their missionary task.

3. Help to establish and sustain meaningful communities of faith for Christians in public life, (in addition to traditional congregational life).

4. Help to devise meaningful forms of spirituality and liturgy and give appropriate pastoral support to lay people as they carry out their duties in their public life.

All this has serious implication for the method and concept of training ordinands in theological colleges. If the ordained ministers of the Church are to succeed in the task outlined above, they will need to be trained to undertake it.

If the Church is to take the ministry of lay people in their public life seriously there must be a fresh appraisal of the way ordained ministers are trained and a massive shift in resources will be required.

The Westhill proposals are likely to meet strong resistance, not only on financial grounds but also from those people who regard the Gospel as mainly a private and individual affair.

Further Needs Identified by the Westhill Consultation

The Westhill Initiative represents an attempt to provide for 'Command Headquarters' a summary of the issues which have to be considered before an effective strategy can be put in place. Two other important points emerged at the Consultation which are summarised below:

1. There should be further study of those forces which shape and influence both society and the Church together with an analysis of the forces which prevent the gospel impingeing on public affairs.

2. There is a particular need to support those groups who face discrimination in public institutions. It was suggested that we should listen to more stories from Christians in public life who might be 'exemplars' of the challenges faced.

There was some ambivalence about the role of the local church. Most people at the consultation agreed that the local congregation was the focal point of worship and community for Christians. However some people felt that the congregation was at present ill-equipped to offer the support needed. The Westhill College initiative was an important step forward.

Great care, however, will have to be taken to ensure that 'authentic' lay people in public life are involved in future consultations otherwise the initiative may become clerically dominated.

It will be important also to involve those support organisations with first hand frontier experience which are already well established. These include important national organisations such as the Comino Foundation of the Royal Society of Arts; St George's House, Windsor Castle; Luton Industrial College; the Christian Association of Business Executives; the Industrial Mission Association and the Industry Churches' Forum.

People and Work Programme

I end this Chapter with a brief description of an initiative taken by 'Command Headquarters' in the Anglican Diocese of Peterborough[2] prompted by the Industrial Mission team. It illustrates a well thought-out attempt to put into practice some of the ideas which emerged at Westhill, though it must be said that the initiative pre-dates the Westhill Consultation!

The initiative in the Diocese of Peterborough is entitled the 'People and Work Programme'. It is a 'lay-led' three year Programme designed to help Christians to live out their faith in the world of work. The Programme utilises and co-ordinates all the existing resources in the Diocese.

Groups are established around the main urban centres of Peterborough, Northampton, Kettering, Wellingborough and Daventry.

The programme is open-ended. It seeks to draw together groups of Christian working people 'with common interests, concerns and needs', and to provide them with resources that will help them to address the issues that they face in their workplace.

There are no recommended patterns for the composition of local groups. Some groups may meet on a regular basis with a programme of activities. Others may want to have 'one-off' events. Some may want to engage in projects which involve members in independent study and research. The ultimate goal, however, is that all Christians, who spend substantial parts of their lives at work, have access to the support and guidance that the programme offers.

Within the flexibility outlined above, various 'menus' are offered including pastoral support, an examination of Christian values, education, prayer and worship, and the multi-faith community.

Pastoral Support
Under this heading are included such subjects as:
Stress Management
Alcohol/Drug abuse
Sexual Harassment
HIV/Aids
Equal Opportunities: Gender, Race, Disability, Age
Special Needs
Personal Relationships
Balance: Work/Social/Service/Family
Change: Employment, Redundancy, New-management

Christian Values
This heading includes topics such as:
The Environment: pollution, ecology, land use, conservation, heritage preservation, transport
Wealth distribution: taxation, benefits, income, budgeting, consumerism, market forces, short-term profit
Power: politics, self determination, ownership, control, promotion

Participation: autonomy/collaboration, autocracy/democracy
Authority: rights and responsibilities

Education
Behind this heading is the Christian concern with the growth
and development of the whole person; body, mind, and spirit,
throughout the whole of life.

Evangelism
Mission and Evangelism embraces:
Personal life stories
Representing Christ in the workplace
Social interaction with non-Christians
Protocol: 'a time and place for everything'
Taking experience of the workplace back into the Church

Prayer and Worship
Groups may engage strategies to:
Devise special services with workplace themes
Write articles from the workplace in parish magazines
Arrange retreats and conferences on spirituality and expression
of faith in the workplace

Multi-Cultural Society
It is recognised that in Britain there are people in communities
and workplaces who are of other faiths as well as no faith
allegiance at all. Christians need to know more about the
world faiths that are prevalent in British Society.

Summary
In the literature provided for the 'People and Work' programme it is emphasised that the range of styles and group
activity is as wide as the issues that may be pursued. They may
include single events, study courses, fixed term projects, ongoing support groups, 'prayer breakfasts' and residential week-
ends.

The 'People at Work' programme in the Diocese of Peterborough is an impressive initiative. In summary I can do no
better than quote from the programme 'Guidelines':

'The ultimate objective is that all Christian people who
work and who are accountable to others in some way for the
quality of goods and services that they provide should have

support and encouragement as they seek to make their secular work become full-time service for God. For those who try to make the whole of their life consistent with the teaching of the Father, the Son and the Holy Spirit, the programme is to be seen as enabling rather than an additional burdensome commitment'.

CHAPTER SIX

Ethics in Public Life – or is it the Law of the Jungle?

People in public life often find that their private lives come under close scrutiny, especially if they seek high office in the political arena. Recent examples have demonstrated how the media can probe into the marital relationships of people in public life both in the United Kingdom and in America. Ordained ministers are not exempt from this scrutiny! However, I want to discuss here, not the private lives of public figures (which may or may not affect their professional judgements) but matters of public ethics and, in particular, Business Ethics which is of particular interest to me as an Industrial Chaplain.

Many books have been written about morality on matters such as sexual relationships. However, there have been far fewer books written about Business Ethics and public morality. Yet this subject is of growing importance. I have listed some of the more recent books in the appendix.

In 1991 there was a huge scandal in the banking world involving bogus loans, theft, bribery and corruption. The bank involved, BCCI was eventually shut down by the Bank of England. Many people thought that BCCI should have been closed much sooner and questions were asked in the House of Commons about the matter. Unfortunately depositors among the Asian community were especially hit by the closure in Britain. It also emerged that some of the managers were religious people and the bank provided a prayer room where some managers were said to pray four or five times a day!

In the same year Robert Maxwell, the head of an enormous business empire, died leaving behind him huge financial difficulties. Investigation into his companies is still proceeding at the time of writing. It appears that Maxwell raided his companies' pension funds to prop up share prices, and the banks are faced with the dilemma of the prospect of confronting the pensioners in the High Court who, understandably, are fighting for their share of the funds.

In 1992 questions were even being raised about the ethics of Lloyds Insurance because it appeared that some Members of Lloyds seemed to be more favourably treated than others.

These examples are exceptional. It might be thought that ethical problems do not arise in most businesses. Indeed when I organised a major conference on Business Ethics in Birmingham during my Presidency of the Rotary Club of Birmingham in 1990–1991, some people criticised the event on the grounds that it was 'preaching to the converted'! Yet any person in business or public life inevitably is faced with ethical problems, sooner or later.

In January 1993, The *Independent on Sunday* published a report of a survey by the University of Westminster. It revealed that many people in Britain would jettison their principles if they affected their companies' profitability. Finance and Marketing directors scored low on the league table of ethics. The climate of opinion was summed up by one respondent: 'In general business ethics does not come up very high in the scale of human behaviour. Professional standards and levels of caring leave a lot to be desired.'[1]

What is Ethics?

Ethics is concerned with values. Ethics deals with matters of right and wrong. Ethics is the process by which people evaluate their actions from the perspective of moral principles. This evaluation may be on the basis of conscience (a 'feeling within' that an action is either right or wrong) or on the basis of traditional religious ideals and convictions. It may be in obedience to a set of moral laws or in other ways. There are a variety of yardsticks which people use. For most of us there is more than ONE set of ideals or moral principles. We are pulled in several directions. Rigid moral judgements based upon those of one individual are not usually to be commended as can be seen from the stories from the front line quoted in chapter four.

It is quite impossible to be involved in business (or public life in any institution) without encountering ethical issues. Moreover these issues are seldom straight forward matters of black or white. It is by no means true to say that good people will always make the right ethical decisions. It is not always obvious what is the right thing to do, even with a cultivated conscience and a prayerful approach to the problems.

Decision-making within public institutions often involves sorting through an immense web of complicated factors. People who are managers are required to manage values and constantly have to make choices between conflicting priorities. This requires great skill. Managing values in public life is of a different dimension to discerning between what is right and what is wrong in private and personal life.

This is not intended to be a text book on Business Ethics and it is not possible to do justice to these questions in this book. Readers are referred to the appendices for further study on Business Ethics.

Suffice it to say that 'doing the right thing' is by no means always an easy matter. Support and advice systems, run by experienced consultants, can be very helpful to those who have to make decisions 'at the front line'.

There are two dimensions to ethical issues in institutions: individual and corporate. These two dimensions may require two corresponding kinds of support systems. At the individual level a simple support group may be all that is necessary to sustain those who seek to apply relevant moral principles to courses of action which appear to conflict with their Christian or moral principles. For corporate issues a more sophisticated support system may be needed.

The Scope of Business Ethics

The scope of Business Ethics is immense. In recent years universities in the United Kingdom (following a similar trend in the United States of America) have begun to establish professorial 'Chairs' of Business Ethics. The subject is far wider than merely keeping a watching brief on accounting procedures or deciding whether or not to open a shop on Sunday. Among subjects discussed in Business Ethics are matters of advertising practice, discrimination in employment practice, responsibility towards customers and local communities, environmental issues, working conditions, use of animal products, investment policies and so on. There are also questions relating to competition and survival.

An American Case Study: The Consequences of Competition

William Diehl, in his book *The Monday Connection*[2] describes how, as a young sales manager, because of his aggressive salesmanship, he enabled his own company to survive during a recession when there was a limited market for a range of products.

One day a competitor telephoned Diehl to ask whether he could arrange a meeting to see if some kind of agreement could be reached between the two companies so that the limited market could be shared between them in some way.

The competitor was a man in his late sixties. American Anti-Trust laws do not permit the meeting between competitors to discuss prices or customers or market share or geographical boundaries. Diehl was also aware of his own responsibility to his company and the wellbeing of his fellow employees.

Yet Diehl was a committed Christian and he felt troubled. His own hard work and competency was apparently driving another company out of business and hurting an old man. When he first began to give the matter some thought he came to the conclusion that he did at least have the option of being less aggressive with his competitor's long-standing customers.

Diehl describes in his book how he took the problem to his pastor. His pastor was unaware of American Anti-Trust laws and kept suggesting ways of arriving at an arrangement.

The pastor was convinced that Diehl had some responsibility towards his competitor. The pastor reminded Diehl about his duty to be 'his brother's keeper', and quoted other biblical texts which gave further trouble to Diehl's conscience.

Diehl's own superior instructed him not to be less aggressive in his salesmanship even with his competitor's long standing customers. If he did less than his best he would be stealing from his own company, the Bethlehem Steel Corporation. He reminded Diehl that a more sensible course of action for the older man who ran the competing company would be to sell the business and retire.

Although this is an American example, it does illustrate the kind of dilemma that Christian lay people face in competitive business in Britain. How do they reconcile Biblical teaching with business life? They are confronted with Biblical texts such as 'Am I my brother's keeper?' (Genesis 4 v9) or more explicit texts such as Leviticus 25 vs 35–37:

'If a fellow Israelite living near you becomes poor and cannot support himself, you must provide for him as you would for a hired man, so that he can continue to live near you . . .'

Young Diehl wrestled with his conscience when he was confronted by these two particular texts.[3] But he learned two important lessons from that experience:

He learned firstly that ordained ministers are not always the most appropriate people to consult when a Christian businessman is trying to relate faith to life at work. Unless ordained ministers have made a study of business issues they will not have the knowledge nor the experience to help.

Secondly Diehl learned that he needed to form a support group of Christians who were competent in their own field of endeavour, to share experience and solicit advice. If an ordained minister were to be a member of such a group, he or she could act as a theological consultant but *not* as leader!

Making Ethical Decisions

It is often assumed that good people will make good decisions. People with good moral principles will naturally act in the right way. That is not always so. In order to make ethical decisions people must have *all* the relevant facts at hand but sometimes it may not be possible to acquire all the facts.

William Diehl, in his book,[4] draws attention to three factors which have to be considered when making ethical decisions:

Firstly, the interests of all those who will be affected by the decision must be respected. Ways should be found to ensure that the action taken will do the most good for most people.

Secondly, individual rights (both legal and moral) must be respected.

Thirdly, the decision must be fair and just.

Rachel Jenkins[5] describes a procedure to analyse what she calls the 'interface' between institutional values and the values of the individuals within institutions. This procedure examines a particular incident which involves conflicting patterns of values and asks the following questions:

1. Who are the main actors in the incident?

2. What aspects in the past have helped to determine the way in which this particular incident is handled ? Are there any 'accepted practices'?

3. Are there any aspects of past practice which may have been suppressed?

4. How is this particular incident linked with the *wider* context in which it is set both in the institution and in society?

5. The fifth question probes the theology behind the incident. What are the signs of hope or redemption in what is happening? What are the signs that human life is being mis-used?

It can be seen from these examples that ethical issues in institutional life are by no means simple and that some support system is required to help Christians to grapple with their dilemmas. It is important to be aware of some potential pitfalls.

Some Pitfalls

When I first became an Industrial Chaplain in 1961, I was frequently greeted by the words, 'Stop swearing everybody – here comes the vicar'. Pin-ups would hastily be hidden, much to my amusement. It was assumed that I disapproved of these things! Ordained ministers have to live down a certain reputation for being 'kill-joys' who go round saying 'Stop it . . . I don't know what you are doing, but stop it!'

There is some justification for this reputation. It can 'rub off' on to all who profess and call themselves Christian! 'We don't know what you are doing, but stop it . . .' Christians can all too easily condemn and come to swift conclusions about ethical issues without knowing all the facts. This is particularly so in matters of ethics in institutions where it is especially important to know *all* the facts. The Church should be very cautious before it lambasts commercial and industrial institutions!

In the summer of 1991 the General Synod of the Church of England decided to endorse a boycott of Nestle Products in the UK in order to protest about the availability of infant formula (baby milk) in Third World countries. The basis for the Synod's vote was the provision of free or subsidised supplies of infant formula to hospitals in the Third World where there are dangers of mixing powdered milk with contaminated water. The circumstances surrounding this case are highly complex and illustrate how outside bodies such as the Church can, with good intentions, make hasty decisions on complicated ethical issues without specialist knowledge of all the facts.

Synod in effect said: 'We don't know what you are doing, but stop it!'

In dealing with ethical issues of this nature it is perhaps wiser to make careful enquiries, and, if possible work from within the organisation with positive sensitivity rather than condemn the organisation from outside by a motion in Synod. Many companies are beginning to use ethical and sociological consultants. Companies welcome the comments of people such as Industrial Chaplains who work alongside the decision makers within the company, sometimes in partnership with other relevant consultative services.

In the United Kingdom Industrial Chaplains are usually invited into a company with the agreement of both management and appropriate employee representatives. This enables them to be able move around the organisation listening, learning and looking in a non-judgemental way. If they do their job properly they are soon able to gain the trust of all concerned and obtain an overview of the entire organisation. In this way, without breaching any confidences, they are able to raise questions in a sensitive and independent manner without necessarily taking sides.

Companies do not operate in a vacuum. Policies of individual companies are frequently influenced by the prevailing economic and ideological climate. Therefore, in addition to an awareness of internal ethical issues it is important also to take note of changing external ideologies. Companies operate within ethical and economic climatic conditions which change frequently!

Changing ideology

Rachel Jenkins, in her booklet *Changing Times, Unchanging Values?*[6] cites examples of changing ideology in the public and private sectors in Britain. She says:

'In the past twelve years we have seen the elevation of the market as the ideal way of regulating all kinds of productive activity. The promotion of market forces as the basis of regulation has profound implications for assessing the quality of work in the public sector, and therefore the resources allocated to that work. The "elevation of the market" has developed alongside a commitment to review public expenditure with the purpose of eliminating "wasteful" expenditure. Cost effectiveness and efficiency have become major issues for those who work in healthcare, education and social services. Previously respected concepts are rejected. Ideals such as compassion or the education of the whole person, body, mind and spirit (not simply for economic productivity) are no longer considered respectable objectives.'

Ideological changes such as the introduction of market forces to regulate the management of schools and the National Health Service disturb and confuse even professional people. Client groups feel powerless to oppose the changes. It seems that ideals such as compassion, encouragement, power-sharing and social justice are now rejected as guiding principles in the face of the encouragement of competition and individualism.

Case Studies to Illustrate Ideological Changes

In her booklet, Rachel Jenkins quotes case studies in Britain:

A Bank[7]

An Assistant Bank Manager had worked in the Bank for twenty years. She took particular pride in making financial affairs accessible to those who were somewhat mystified by them and she encouraged her staff to be helpful and respectful to all customers. Then came changes in central policy and a shift from customer to shareholder interests. She perceived that the bank's new insistence on charging for every piece of extra work or advice was detrimental to the customer and in the long run detrimental to the bank as well. She anticipated the time when she would be faced with the necessity to act against her principles or refuse to do as directed. If she chose the latter course she would put her position at risk. She faced difficult questions of personal integrity and compromise.

A Manufacturing Company[8]

A Christian working in the private sector as financial director of a company described his own motives as 'loving and sharing' whilst he regarded the majority of his colleagues as 'self-seeking and self-centred'. He was highly committed to collaborative ways of managing the firm.

This ideal led him to persuade his colleagues to hold management team meetings and to develop the company according to collaborative principles rather than a 'combative' style. Moreover the company became profitable.

These case studies raise questions about the kind of support needed by those at the 'front line' who have to maintain their energy to keep going, sometimes in the face of opposition.

Corporate Ethics

The increasing emphasis upon market forces was one of the issues that kept recurring during my sabbatical in California. There is a remarkable similarity between America's 'Reagan years' and Britain's 'Thatcher years'.

The importance of individual freedom is written into the American Constitution. The virtues of individual responsibility and individual initiative are praised in American society. Yet just as people who 'pull themselves up with their own boot-straps' are applauded and praised, so those who do not (or cannot for whatever reason) are blamed for their plight.

The result is that America has an unprecedented high standard of living for millions of people, but in the process of making many rich, millions of people are left behind.

Berkeley, where I stayed, is in the San Francisco Bay area. The city may not be typical. It is an area with lovely houses, inhabited mostly by wealthy white people in a beautiful setting in the hills looking over the Bay. Yet on the pavements of the streets in the downtown area of the City are hundreds of homeless people. Every twenty yards there are beggars asking passers-by for 'change'. This situation is worse than London and reminded me in many respects of my visit to Calcutta some years previously!

Few of the homeless people in Berkeley are white. As in Birmingham, England, there is a rich variety of races in California, but many of the non whites seem to have been left behind in the advancing American economic progress. Sadly, since my stay in California a terrible fire has swept through much of that beautiful hillside residential area in Berkeley and three thousand houses were destroyed.

In 1986 the American Roman Catholic Bishops issued a Pastoral Letter entitled *Economic Justice for All* addressed to the 'Principalities and Powers of America'. It was a bold attempt to influence public policy. In that letter the Bishops cited six moral principles:[9]

1. 'Every economic decision and every economic institution must be judged in the light of whether it protects or undermines the dignity of the human person. We judge any economic system by what it does for and to people and by how it permits all to participate in it.

2. Human dignity can be realized and protected only in community. The human person is not only sacred but also social. The command to 'love our neighbour' requires a broad social commitment to the common good.

3. All people have a right to participate in the economic life of society.

4. All members of society have a special obligation to the poor and vulnerable. From the scriptures and church teaching we learn that the justice of a society is tested by the treatment of the poor.

5. Human rights are the minimum conditions for life in community, i.e. all people have a right to life, food, clothing, shelter, rest, medical care, education, employment.

6. Society as a whole, acting through public and private institutions, has the moral responsibility to enhance human dignity and protect human rights. Government has an essential responsibility in this area.'

The preface to the Bishops' Pastoral letter ends with these words:
    'We suggest that the time has come for a "New American Experiment" – to implement economic rights, to broaden the sharing of economic power, and to make economic decisions more accountable to the common good.'
    In compiling the Pastoral letter the Bishops took great care to consult very widely. They listened to all voices in a spirit of mutual respect and open dialogue. As in the English *Faith in the City* Report, the Bishops used the government's own statistics.
    There are many similarities between the American Bishops' Pastoral Letter and the English *Faith in the City* Report. Both documents made a great impact and both dealt with macro economic and corporate ethical issues.
    But words are not enough.
    How can it be ensured that the recommendations contained in these important documents are not lost or left to gather dust on forgotten bookshelves?
    This matter came sharply into focus as a result of the riots which took place in Los Angeles in 1992. Commenting on these riots President George Bush said:
    'It is the system which perpetuates poverty, failure and despair'.[10] The President's statement is an important admission in a society which extols the virtue of individualism. We shall explore some of the ways in which systems and institutions can be transformed in chapter nine. But first we shall explore more fully the tensions in which individuals find themselves at the front line.

CHAPTER SEVEN

Stress at Work

At the front line in times of war soldiers experience extreme forms of stress. They are highly trained and carefully chosen for their tasks and yet they suffer from traumas of many kinds. Compared with the military front line it might be thought that the front line at work or in public life is a peaceful life. It is not! Bill Jordan once told me of the stress he experienced as a trade union official: telephones ringing, people coming and going, the conflicting expectations of workers, managers, the media and the public![1]

In 1992, *The Independent* newspaper reported that the mental health charity, MIND, had published a survey entitled *Stress at Work*.[2] The survey revealed very high levels of stress among people employed in all kinds of work. Fears of redundancy, fears about the recession (which was a severe economic problem in 1992) and anxieties about ability to perform to a high standard of work, were overtaking domestic 'personal' problems as the main causes of stress, particularly in the south of England. Hitherto bereavement, divorce and moving house had been seen as the top stress initiators in Britain.

Two thirds of those who took part in the survey were company directors or managers, people generally considered to have achieved a high degree of job security.

Ms Liz Stayce, MIND's policy director, was reported[2] as saying that time off work because of stress-related illness cost Britain £7bn a year. One hundred and nine companies were surveyed – 31% said that pressure to perform was the biggest factor contributing to stress; 29% said it was fear of redundancy and 29% said it was the recession. Lord Ennals, joint President of MIND, in a foreword to the report, emphasised the importance of companies, both large and small, recognising and dealing with stress. The survey found that 24% of companies used the services of professional internal counsellors and 35% referred staff to external counsellors.

What is Stress?

The *Shorter Oxford Dictionary* defines stress as 'the physical strain or pressure exerted upon a material object'. In physical sciences, pressure is essential to effect change and development. In designing a bridge the various stresses are kept in balance. In the same way, some degree of balanced stress is an essential ingredient for human growth and achievement. Not all stress is bad. Men and women can benefit from a certain amount of stress. We should not want to remove all stress from executives at the front line but we do need to distinguish good forces from bad forces. We need to keep the forces in balance and avoid malignant pressures which can be destructive. We need to encourage healthy pressures.

Occupational psychologist, Alistair Ostell, describes stress as 'the state of affairs which exists when the way people attempt to manage their problems, taxes or exceeds their coping resources'. In this definition stress is not simply derived from an external problem. It is derived from a person's internal coping mechanism. We should therefore be concerned about the way people cope with their problems. Dr Ostell says:

'It is the dysfunctional ways of thinking about themselves and their problems which distresses people more than their lack of technical competence to handle problems'.[4] But Dr Ostell seems to agree that a certain amount of stress is a good thing and that positive management of stress can enable people to work at their most productive capacity.

Two kinds of pressures can therefore be identified. There are the external organisational pressures, and the internal pressures within each individual person. It is not easy to distinguish clearly between these pressures when considering stress at work.

Organisational Pressures

Ivor Capel and John Gurnsey in their book *Managing Stress*[5] point to four key areas which contribute to stress at work:

1. Environmental factors. These include such things as noise, poor lighting conditions and inadequate ventilation, fumes, overcrowding or isolation and badly designed furniture.

2. Job design factors such as conflicting objectives, too much or too little work, monotonous or repetitive work, under-utilisation of skills, too little or too much supervision, lack of involvement and an inability to participate in decision making, inadequate breaks, and (a modern phenomenon) constant use of visual display screens! Under this heading might also be included, anxiety about ability to perform to the standards required by the organisation.

3. Contractual factors. These may include low pay, shift work, unsocial hours and excessive overtime, to which we can add job insecurity, lack of recognition, and poorly thought-out or obscure promotional procedures. Fears about redundancy and the effects of recession also come under this heading. Executives also suffer from stress due to their frequent jetting across the world.

4. Relationship factors. Poor relationships with colleagues, impersonal treatment, sexism or racism and poor communication.

Certain work-related situations can be particularly stressful. Mergers and takeovers can send shivers throughout a company. In the course of my experience as an industrial chaplain I can think of an example where one company was taken over five times within two years. One executive said to me, 'It's all right for you, padre, you know who you work for. We don't!'

Redundancy and the threat of redundancy can be very stressful. It can have an effect similar to that of a bereavement. Redundancy programmes also cause stress to those who administer them. It ought also to be said, however, that in some instances where the work has been particularly stressful, redundancy may come as a great relief! Relocation too can be very stressful. One of my own sons was moved from Wimbledon to Hammersmith, then to Gloucester and from there to Manchester, all within the space of a few months.

In industries where there is the constant introduction of new technologies the associated rapid and constant changes are a major cause of stress. Similarly the continual changes in government policy within the education service have contributed to low morale and a massive exodus from the teaching profession.

Harmful, malignant pressures within institutions may include the content of the actual work people are given to do and their ability to do it. In an ideal situation, the work assigned to a person should equal that person's capacity to do it. There should be equilibrium. If this equilibrium is not achieved or if it is disturbed there is a potential harmful stress situation.

People are sometimes required to do work beyond their capability and may try to 'cover up' their inability to cope. It is not unusual to find executives promoted beyond their capacities. This phenomenon is called 'The Peter Principle'. Sometimes executives suffer breakdown as a result of this stress. It is not always easy for an organisation to demote ineffective executives. Unhappily, there is often far less attention paid to broken-down executives than to broken-down machinery both in terms of maintenance and repair.

Sometimes the scope of work fails to match the capacity of the person who does it. The classic example of this state of affairs existed in the motor car industry for many years. Highly intelligent people were employed on the 'track' doing repetitive and boring mundane work under 'payments by results' or 'measured day work' systems. The result was a highly strike prone industry. The workforce began to attack the organisation. Certain enlightened car companies in the 1970s, e.g. Volvo and Saab began to introduce Job Enrichment programmes and even abandoned the 'track' in an attempt to remedy this problem. The modern philosophy of 'Total Quality' is a more recent attempt to utilise the full skills of the workforce.

Pressures from Within: Personality Factors

In addition to external pressures from the institution there are pressures from within each individual. Long ago Freud detected basic libidinal and aggressive feelings latent within each individual, whether expressed or not. These feelings are common to everyone. They are a basic part of our human make-up. Libidinal needs for love, affection, acceptance – and feelings of dependence are natural to every human being. Emotional drives can be used positively and creatively. They can be engines for productive efficiency.

However, in British society there seems to be a 'taboo' about the expression of feelings. It is considered inappropriate for people to express their feelings at work, so these feelings can become bottled up. They are unable to be used to their full potential as engines for creative and productive capacity.

In recent times it is beginning to be realised that we need to create a climate within institutions where feelings and emotions are recognised and can be expressed. We are beginning to rediscover the importance of creating legitimate opportunities to talk about problems and frustrations at work. This is at least as important as creating opportunities to talk about the effective use of machinery or about sales policy. We need healthy organisations which minimise malignant pressures upon people. It is possible to construct model organisations where feelings can be expressed in a *non-risk situations*. The Co-Counselling Community[6] in America, and more recently in Britain, has pioneered such models. Here there is an enormous latent opportunity for the Christian Church!

Symptoms of Stress

Commenting upon the 1992 MIND report on *Stress at Work*, *The Independent* newspaper in a leading article said:[7]

'Stress exists. Its classic symptoms are sleeplessness, outbursts of anger and an inability to concentrate. It may result in under-performance or absenteeism and ultimately in breakdown.'

It is therefore important to detect malignant stress in its early stages bearing in mind that the causes may be both organisational and personal. Both external as well as internal factors must be considered. It is of little use laying the blame on individual inadequacies if the organisational structure is at fault. No amount of counselling can cure malignant organisational structures. In identifying symptoms of stress, the Institute of Personnel Management in their Stress Management Fact Sheet No.7 suggests that there are certain changes of mood; cognitive changes; and behavioural changes to look for:

'Changes of mood to identify include anger, irritability, bitterness and resentment. People may feel anxious or even have feelings of panic, hopelessness, sadness or depression when under too much stress.

Cognitive changes may include difficulty in concentrating, difficulty in making decisions, trouble in remembering things and an inability to "switch off" even when trying to relax or sleep.

Behavioural changes include absenteeism, dependence upon drugs or alcohol, excessive doublechecking. People under too much stress often take longer over normal tasks and habitually make errors.'

The Reverend G.C. Harding in a lecture at a conference sponsored by Coventry Industrial Mission,[8] pointed out that nature has provided natural biological defence mechanisms which come to our aid in the face of danger. The tom cat arches its back and spits when faced with an enemy. The 'nice' executive cannot do this, yet the human body has a natural inclination to react in a similar way to the tom cat. We need to recognise this instinctive reaction. Human beings need to make use of natural defence mechanisms when under stress and not pretend that they do not exist.

Flight or Fight?

Some animals, when hunted, 'freeze' into the background and sometimes even change their colour in order to blend into their surroundings until danger passes. This mechanism is also part of our human make-up. Sometimes a person under stress feels 'hypnotised', 'caught in a trap', 'frozen to the spot'. These feelings are symptoms of stress: nature has come to our aid. The 'switch off' mechanism is an important defence.

Harding points out that mankind's genius (over and above the animals) lies in an ability not only to express feeling of anger, e.g. spit like the tom cat, or run away from the problem or 'freeze', but to be able to switch behaviour to something more creative. Mankind's salvation does not come by being saved from a situation (which may lead only to self-denial and self-hatred) but in dealing with situations realistically.

Prevention and Cure

In seeking prevention and cure it is necessary to deal with both the external organisational factors and the internal personality factors. Speaking at the Industrial Mission conference on Stress, Robert de Board, (at that time a member of the Administrative Staff College at Henley on Thames), told delegates that a strategy is needed to enable organisations to be more 'people-centred'.[9] In terms of company policy we need to encourage senior managers to sit down with colleagues to see what standards are wanted, how these standards can be achieved in the company, and to ask basic questions about the causes of unacceptable levels of stress in the working situation and what action can be taken to reduce corrosive pressures within the organisation. In other words, an analysis should be made of the stress problems that exist in the organisation.

In effecting prevention and cure it is also helpful for people to 'know themselves'! Organisations may use various personality tests for this purpose. It has been said, rather flippantly, that the psychotic personality builds castles in the air, the neurotic personality lives in them and the psychologists collect the rents!

The Institute of Personnel Management Fact Sheet[10] points out that certain characters seem to be more susceptible to levels of stress than others. The distinction has been made between Type A and Type B personalities. Type A personalities do too many things at once, they talk and drive fast, they have a consistent sense of urgency and are often hyper-aggressive. They are workaholics and their interior chemistry drives them to take on more and more work, irrespective of whether the organisation in which they work expects this of them. Type A personalities are more likely to suffer from stress than Type B personalities, who take life in a more care-free and leisurely style.

Industrial Chaplains often find themselves used as a help

line. Yet, as the MIND report recommends, sometimes more professional and systematic help is required. For example, in a company where certain employees must be away from home frequently, careful monitoring of recruitment is needed to eliminate those who may not be able to cope with this kind of stress. Other positive practical steps such as the introduction of flexible working hours can help to relieve the stress of commuting. Some companies have set up creches to help parents with young children who wish to continue working.

But, perhaps above all, there is a need for balance between work and rest. Modern society, with its feverish activity, seems to have lost this balance. A balance between labour and rest is required both for organisational and individual reasons. The 'Keep Sunday Special' group is a lobby for organisational sanity. It is also a lobby for individual health.

I conclude this chapter with a plea that individuals at the front line should take time to relax. Simple relaxation techniques are a necessary skill for all who work in the front line in this modern world.

The ancient Hebrews realised the importance of the balance between labour and rest. They realised also the importance of being able to tune in to the rhythm of nature. As night follows day, so rest follows work. Above all the Hebrews emphasised the need for a whole day of Sabbath rest within the seven-day working week, because God himself rested from his creative work on the seventh day.

It is not without significance that the Old Testament word for 'faith' means 'lying on the ground'. It is an attitude of spiritual rest. We shall think about this further in a later chapter on 'Spirituality at the Front Line'. Suffice it to say now that just as within every human being there are those libidinal forces identified by Freud, so there are also inner spiritual resources. Human beings need to be able to tap those resources. Spiritual growth occurs when time is set aside for the real needs of living and the art of relaxation is taken seriously. Some people would advocate yoga and meditation. The experience and the joy of massage is to be commended. There are 'hang-ups' about massage because it sometimes has a 'bad press' but massage can be very therapeutic, especially if soft music is played! Massage helps in the process of self-knowledge and self-acceptance.

'Know thyself'. This is an oft quoted piece of advice. Essentially it is the process of discovering what it is to be a real human being, and discovering the importance of self love in the true sense of that word. Perfect love casts out fear. When we are no longer afraid of ourselves and our inner libidinal drives, we can become more understanding of other people and more tolerant of the strains and stresses of the world around us. We can admit our faults and accept the failures of others.

> Dear Lord and Father of mankind,
> Forgive our foolish ways!
> Re-clothe us in our rightful mind,
> In purer lives thy service find,
> In deeper reverence praise.
>
> Drop thy still dews of quietness,
> Till all our strivings cease;
> Take from our souls the strain and stress,
> And let our ordered lives confess
> The beauty of thy peace.[11]

CHAPTER EIGHT

The 'Sunday–Monday' Connection

One of my earliest experiences as a young Industrial Chaplain was to enter a busy executive's office. I tapped nervously on the door and entered the great man's room. He appeared to be answering two telephones at once and dictating memos at the same time. I felt immediately that I was intruding and prepared to beat a hasty retreat but he held his hand up as I was about to disappear and pointed to an empty chair. I sat there for about ten minutes whilst he dealt with the phone calls and the memos. Then he got up, put the 'engaged' notice on his door and instructed his secretary that he should not be interrupted. He then began to pour out his frustrations onto me whilst I sat there. He talked for about twenty minutes. I nodded, grunted, but said very little. He then thanked me very much and said, 'Please come and see me again.' I suppose I acted as a kind of 'waste paper basket' for him. That early experience as an Industrial Chaplain taught me a great deal. It is an experience which has been repeated hundreds of times since then.

Busy executives, and people in similar pressured positions, need someone that they can trust to talk to and act as a safe waste paper basket into which they can put their 'trash'. They also need someone, like an Industrial Chaplain, who knows the company but is not 'of' the company. They need a mentor and confidant.

The Servant Society in Santa Barbara, California, USA, provides this resource to senior executives in business and government. Very often executives, for reasons of confidentiality, cannot share their decision making concerns with their peers. In the United Kingdom, Industrial Chaplains, by virtue of their regular visits to companies and their knowledge of economic affairs, often find themselves in this role, as I have described. This is a skilled task, but there are not enough Industrial Chaplains available to visit more than a fraction of those work places that would welcome them. Neither, for a variety of reasons, are there adequate outside resources of other kinds yet available to those who find themselves at the 'front line'.

Support Groups

William Diehl, in his book *The Monday Connection* describes how he gathered round himself a Christian support group in his American home town.[1] Diehl recommends Occupational support groups – made up of competent practitioners working in the same or similar fields of work. He says that an optimum group consists of from six to twelve people who have made a commitment to each other to meet on a regular basis for the purpose of sharing their experience and concerns as they try to live out their faith in their daily lives. Confidentiality is essential. Without confidentiality, a support group cannot function.

It is not wise for the groups to be composed of people working within the same organisation since there is always the risk that somebody will violate confidentiality. There is also the danger that Christian support groups within a single organisation can be 'taken over' and become holy huddle groups!

The support group to which Diehl belonged was known as the 'Monday Connection' – hence the title of his book. The group met for breakfast on the first Monday of each month. For each monthly session one of the members volunteered to present a real-life occupational case study. Members of the group never passed judgement on what was said. They were encouraged to examine as many options as possible in the case study. The role of the ordained minister (if present) was to listen and to offer appropriate biblical and theological insights.

In the 'Monday Connection' group, the person who presented the case study was also asked to pay close attention during Sunday worship the day before for any 'connections'. Did any elements of the Sunday worship (such as lessons, prayers, sermon) connect with the case study? If so, how? This aspect of the group sometimes led the ordained minister present to pay more attention to the actual needs of the congregation and to devise more relevant forms of Sunday worship!

Training in Listening Skills

Members of support groups need help to develop their listening skills. This is an important task for the Church. Sometimes listening is all that is required to meet a particular need as I discovered early in my experience as an Industrial Chaplain.

There is an important distinction between 'conversation' and sensitive 'attention'. People sometimes do not listen or pay adequate attention to each other. They make speeches at each other based upon their own emotional needs. For similar reasons, clergy may sometimes fail to 'listen' to the needs of their congregation because they have their own preconceived agendas! This is frequently the reason why Sunday worship fails to 'connect' with Monday needs.

Whilst in California I met Dottie Wylie, the Adult Education and Training Officer in the Episcopal Diocesan Office, San Francisco. She made the point that it is not just a question of 'firing up' a congregation in Church on Sunday and then 'sending them out to live and work to the praise and glory of God' without also following up the worship and the prayers with other kinds of support. It is important to provide opportunities for people in the congregation to reflect together upon their day-to-day secular experiences, talk about these experiences, listen to each other, and to relate theological and biblical insights to the issues raised. This is not easy, but then nor is it easy to struggle alone!

Dottie Wylie said that ordained ministers should use Confirmation Classes and Adult Education classes for this purpose. Bible study should be set within the context of personal experience. It is important to start from where people ARE. What is their job? Does it bring satisfaction? If not, why not? What does it feel like to lose a job? An examination of the context of actual experience, whether it is fulfilling or soul destroying, should precede any biblical insights that may be provided by a text. For similar reasons evangelism cannot be effective unless Faith relates to Life. Preaching the Gospel 'at' people is not enough. This insight has important implications for the Decade of Evangelism.

Lesslie Newbigin makes the same point in his book *The Gospel in a Pluralist Society*.[2] He writes:

'Contemporary theological debate has highlighted the role of experience as providing the contemporary context within which alone the message of scripture and tradition has to be grasped.'

Context before Text

It is helpful to provide various ways to enable people 'at the front line' to tell their story, relate the context of their day to day work, receive support from their fellow Christians, be equipped with the insights of biblical tradition, and be inspired by a relevant spirituality.

In some churches, lay people are encouraged to 'tell their story' publicly. They are given opportunity to address the congregation in place of the usual sermon by the ordained minister in Sunday worship. Several of the stories quoted in chapter four of this book were told in this way. A course of such addresses may be particularly helpful during Lent. Such a course, given by appropriate people from the congregation, may include the following topics:

> A Christian in Business
> A Christian in Politics
> A Christian in Local Government
> A Christian in the Health Service
> A Christian Housewife and Parent
> A Christian School Teacher, etc.

It is helpful, after the service, to provide coffee and, if possible, leave time for opportunity to discuss the content of the address. In this process the importance of sensitive listening skills is especially important, otherwise further frustration (rather than support) will result. So there does need to be careful preparation before such a course of addresses is given, and the ordained minister should give an explanation of the purpose of the course.

A Relevant Liturgy

It is of little use providing these kinds of opportunities unless the liturgy itself is relevant to the day-to-day life of those who worship. There is a separate chapter on Liturgy for the front line later in this book, but a few simple points should be noted. It is sometimes helpful if, on each Sunday, a visual symbol representing one aspect of daily life at the 'front line' can be brought up to the altar table with the Offertory. In some churches members of the congregation bring up to the altar objects from their daily work – such as a desk-top computer, a political banner, duster and chalk, dust-pan and brush, etc. At the same time, the intercessions should include prayers for those who create wealth, those who serve in political life, schools, colleges or hospitals or whatever is especially appropriate for the address given on that day.

This can all be 'window dressing' unless the organisational structure of the Church itself is appropriate. If the Church remains a kind of holy club, drawing members into itself and measuring success in terms of numbers in the Sunday congregation or money put on the plate, the world of Church and the real world at the front line will continue to be 'worlds apart'.

Alternative Communities of Faith

Dianna Crabtree in her important book *Empowering the Laity*[3] suggests that every aspect of Church organisational life needs to be examined in order to clarify the contribution it makes to what she calls 'the empowerment of Lay Ministry'. This examination may lead to the design of new organisational structures for the congregation and initiate new ways of being 'the Church'.

Dianna Crabtree describes in her book how one parish set up a comprehensive programme of Adult Residential Conferences which extended over a period of several years in order to achieve this.

In the first year the conference took the theme 'Discovering our gifts'. In the second year the parish began to tackle practical planning processes and to restructure the organisational life of the Church. The third annual conference discussed the theme 'Beyond Sunday Christianity'.

In year four, a Laity 'Listening Team' was formed. This listening team was then put to work!

A typical group listening session embraced the following steps:

1. Describe how you spend your day.

2. What satisfies you at work? What dissatisfies you at work? What is stressful?

3. What is the impact of your work upon your health? your family? your financial life?

4. What changes would you recommend in your own work-place?
To what extent can you help (or not help)?

5. What are the issues that you deal with in your workplace? Are they just and fair?

6. Does it make any difference that you are a Christian in your workplace? How does faith relate to work?

Ordained ministers were encouraged to take part in these listening groups as consultants.

Sector Ministry

In modern life, people are frequently asked 'who are you?'. But there is a question behind the question.

The question really is 'what job do you do?' As a young man I could answer 'I am a bank clerk', or 'I am a wireless mechanic in the Royal Air Force'.

People are defined and valued in modern society by the job they do. This is one reason why it is particularly painful to be unemployed because an unemployed person when asked the question 'who are you?' can feel that he or she is a 'nobody'.

The issues surrounding employment and unemployment are therefore of crucial importance in modern society and deserve very special attention from the Christian Church. That is why in Britain and in many places elsewhere in the world, Industrial Chaplains have been appointed.

One of the chief tasks of Industrial Chaplains in Britain is to acquire practical knowledge and experience of the commercial and industrial world, by regularly visiting companies and work places, 'networking' management and trade union organisations, reading, study, and attending appropriate conferences arranged by secular institutions. Chaplaincies to business organisations are usually arranged on an ecumenical basis and after full consultation with management and employees organisations.

Industrial Chaplains 'walk the shop floor' regularly and make a special effort to get to know key people at all levels within the organisation. As well as offering a traditional pastoral ministry, they seek to minister to those people who are decision makers, and are sometimes able to participate in training programmes and act in a consultative capacity. Much depends upon the skills, sensitivity and personality of the chaplain, and the trust built up over a period of many years.

Most Industrial Chaplains take specialist qualifications such as a Diploma in Personnel Management or Business Administration. Industrial Chaplains listen very carefully to the people they meet as they visit companies. They are careful not to do most of the talking! Industrial Chaplains attach great importance to a 'listening ministry' . . . listening to the world, (in this instance the economic world) and relating theology and biblical insights to the issues raised in the economic world. Even so, Industrial Chaplains recognise the pitfalls of clerical dominance!

Much of the work of Industrial Chaplains has tended to be low key and has lacked publicity. This is a pity because Industrial Mission has a very important part to play in empowering lay people for ministry at the front line.

Alongside Industrial Chaplains (and other sector ministries such as University Chaplains, School Chaplains, Hospital Chaplains, Police Chaplains, etc.) is another important group of ordained ministers who can offer support to lay people at the front line. These are those ordained Ministers who are themselves employed in secular work. In the Anglican Church such ministers are known as 'non stipendiary ministers' or 'ministers in secular employment'.

It must be said, however, that frequently non-stipendiary

ministers are simply seen by the Church as a resource to supplement 'parochial' and 'congregational' ministries. This may divert energy away from their task of thinking through what it actually means to be a priest (if such they are) incarnate in secular life. It is much easier for men (and women!) to express their priesthood within the setting of a local congregation than it is to express their priesthood as a manager within a large store or company.

It is therefore important that non-stipendiary ministers themselves receive appropriate support for their front-line task, otherwise the Church might be in danger of under-utilising a very valuable human resource.

Some years ago I was asked by the Bishop of Coventry to act as a mentor to one of the non-stipendiary ministers in his Diocese who was an executive with a large multi-national company. We still meet regularly. I have considered it an immense privilege to undertake this task. I encourage him to 'tell his story' (which is included in chapter four of this book) and to relate biblical and theological insights to the various issues that emerge in his daily experience as an executive with the company. Some pressures that he has had to face have conflicted with his Christian convictions. It has not been easy for him because the company has had to rationalise many departments, due in part to the recession. It seemed, at one stage, that he would, like many of his executive colleagues, join the ranks of the unemployed!

He told me what one of his colleagues said to him as the day approached for the redundancies to be announced:

'It will be all right for you, because you are also a priest!'

Would it have been 'all right'? Whilst non-stipendiary ministers in the Anglican Church may not have an 'identity crisis' when faced with redundancy from a secular firm, they nonetheless face a crisis in other ways. It would seem that non stipendiary ministers may sometimes require more concrete forms of support from the Church in the form of financial or even legal aid. At times of recession, they are no more secure from redundancy than their colleagues. But this is what 'Incarnational Priesthood' is all about.

In this chapter I have illustrated a few examples of support structures for lay people at the front line of public life, particularly in secular employment, they have all been of a comparatively simple nature, designed to cope with what I have called 'micro' issues.

However, as I have already hinted in this chapter, there are frequently more sophisticated forces at work which require a more sophisticated support system for those involved 'at the front line'. I will describe examples of these in the next chapter but first I want to describe another method of support at the front line: the Covenant.

Covenant Groups

Covenant groups are fairly common in America. In one parish ten members of the parish have covenanted together to spend a whole year focusing on 'Faith and Work' issues.

The year's programme has comprised of:

An autumn retreat using Myers Briggs techniques[4] together with worship and meditation as an aid to cementing the group together in a covenant relationship. The autumn programme also included further sessions on 'self discovery in context' and the development of listening skills.

During the winter months the covenant group studied some basic ideas about ministry including some techniques for evaluating opportunities for ministry at the front line.

In the spring the group studied the 'macro' factors in economic life, market forces, the factors which lead to recession and unemployment, wealth creation and wealth distribution and the principalities and powers in high places. All this is part and parcel of the context of their day-to-day life in the front line.

Self Development: pressures and expectations

I shall make a brief comment from my own experience about 'self development'. Self development does not take place in a vacuum. We frequently behave very differently in different contexts and roles. As a young man I commuted from the London suburbs into the West End in a crowded suburban train each day. From the moment I set foot in the crowded railway carriage surrounded by business people with newspapers and rolled umbrellas and bowler hats, I realised that I was a different person to the young man who had left home a quarter of an hour previously! I was employed by the National

Provincial Bank in their Trafalgar Square branch. The pressures and the expectations were of a completely changed dimension to those of a homeloving son or member of my parish church choir! My role did not alter again until I stepped out of the train and caught the bus home at the end of a long working day.

I realise that this experience, together with my experience as an Air Wireless Mechanic in the Royal Air Force, played an important part in my own self development. I thank God for the support I received at this formative stage of my life within those institutions.

In this chapter I have illustrated a few examples of support structures for lay people at the front line. The support structures have mainly been of a simple nature designed to cope with what I have called 'micro' issues. It is comparatively easy to find a mentor or to form a support or covenant group. This can be done from a local congregational base, though as we have seen it is better still if the congregation itself can be restructured to focus more clearly on this task of 'empowering the laity'.

However, as I have already hinted in this chapter there are 'macro' factors at work in the secular world. To understand these factors and to manage large organisations which are increasingly multi-national requires a more sophisticated support system. I discovered examples of such support structures in California and there are a number of parallel examples in the United Kingdom. I describe some of these in the next chapter.

CHAPTER NINE

Transforming Institutions

Roles

In the previous chapter we described the ways in which people behave differently in different roles. The same people may behave very differently in their role as parents in their family life at home to the way they behave in their public role, e.g. as a Cabinet Minister in Government or as a Senior Civil Servant, or as a business or professional person. I described, how as a young man, my own behaviour patterns changed dramatically as I boarded the commuter train bound for the office in London every morning. There seems to be a 'split' between private and public modes of human behaviour.

People such as medical practitioners (particularly if they are specialists) can be charming and friendly people as private individuals at home or even in church. But the same person, in the professional white coat, can walk briskly down a hospital corridor and completely ignore his next door neighbour or closest friend as the 'public role' is assumed! Clergy and undertakers are likely to adopt different modes of behaviour when they assume their roles in public life: the sympathetic look, the pious voice, is put on almost unconsciously! The school teacher can relax in the staff room with colleagues but assumes a completely different character in the corridor or classroom. There are often very good reasons for these behaviour patterns, not least for self protection!

Allied to this phenomenon is the fact that modern society frequently identifies and values people by the role they perform in public life. When asked 'Who are you?' people reply, 'I am a doctor' or 'I am a teacher'. Society identifies and rewards people by their job. Because of this, redundancy and unemployment can be devastating for an individual.

It is sometimes assumed that roles are relatively superficial. They are 'put on' and 'taken off' as we would put on and take off clothes. It is assumed that just as beneath the clothes is the naked self so beneath the 'role' is the 'true self'. This view is too simplistic.

Professor Robert Bellah, in his book, *The Good Society* points out that people internalise their roles. If a person's role is removed, there does not remain the 'true self' but instead there remains an impoverished remnant of the true self. This is where the sociological concept of living within 'institutions' is very significant.

Institutions

Human beings do not live in isolation. We live within institutions. Every role that we assume is deeply embedded within an 'institution'. The word institution can be misunderstood to mean simply something like a hostel or a state run nursing home or a prison! However Robert Bellah uses this word much more widely in a sociological sense meaning the 'patterned ways which human beings have developed in order to live together'.[1] Institutions have a powerful influence on those who operate within them.

Thus, the role of the father or mother is embedded in the institution of the family. The institution of the family shapes and forms the parental role. Similarly, the role of a doctor is embedded in the medical institution; that of civil servants in the civil service; that of clergymen in the Church, and so on.

Bellah says that various institutional spheres – the economy, politics, the family, etc – 'embody and specify culturally transmitted ultimate values in terms of what is right and wrong, good and bad'.[2] Because we live our lives in and through institutions, it is necessary that we take some responsibility for institutions and seek to change them if necessary. Moreover, because of the power of institutions to influence and form the human beings within them, we should seek, if need be, to transform the institutions which form US! Institutions are not unchangeable.

It used to be thought (and sometimes still is thought!) that institutions are 'given' and cannot be changed – 'as it was in the beginning, is now and ever shall be, world without end . . .' This is not true. So, for example, monastic institutions were constantly reformed throughout their history. Those who talk about the values inherent in the traditional family sometimes fail to realise how even family life has changed over the centuries. The emergence of the one-parent family or the 'gay' family may need to be seen in this context. All changes are not necessarily for the better. Changes have to be evaluated and criteria have to be established for what constitutes the 'good' institution for each age.

Another complicating factor is that institutions inter-act with one another. Some institutions seek to limit the power and influence of other institutions. In economic life, institutions compete with one another. Lloyds Bank competes with Barclays. The Ford Motor Company competes with the Rover Group. Furthermore some institutions may seek to be more 'moral' than others. It was fascinating to see how various companies took their stand concerning the Sunday trading issue. Whilst some companies openly disregarded the law and wanted total de-regulation, others resolutely refused to open on Sunday until the law permitted them to do so. At the time of the free vote in the House of Commons in December 1993 a coalition of retailers, led by Marks and Spencer, proposed that restrictions should be based upon certain types of shop and that there should only be unrestricted opening on the four Sundays before Christmas for all shops.

What is the relevance of all this to 'ministry in the market place'?

It is twofold.

Firstly, because of the powerful formative influence of

institutions (including their power to shape values) and because institutions may even sometimes become corrupt, people within them need 'independent' support. But they need more than this.

Secondly, institutions themselves need constant evaluation, reformation and transformation. For this to happen considerable expertise is required. Institutions can be reformed from within but we must never underestimate the influence of public opinion, public debate and the prophetic power of pressure groups, political parties and religious groups to transform institutions from without!

In this process therefore the Church has a very important part to play both in supporting 'front line' people within institutions and encouraging (from the outside) any necessary institutional reforms.

In all this, it has to be remembered that the Church is an institution (with all that implies) and therefore the Church itself may need to be reformed if it is be effective in its task of reforming secular institutions! The Church as an institution has within it all the forces that lead to inertia ... Recent debates within the institutional Church about women priests and gay priests graphically illustrate this problem. These are difficult issues but if the Church diverts its energy to these internal matters it may have less energy for effective evangelism and support for lay people in their 'front line' ministries.

The Consortium Model

Whilst institutional reform of the Christian Church may be desirable, in practice this may not be possible in the short term! So in the meantime it is important to look at some of the models which have been set up which involve the Church in an attempt to influence and transform policies in secular institutions. Readers should consult the appendices for a more comprehensive list but at this point I shall describe just a few examples.

One way of influencing policies of institutions is to form an alliance or consortium in order to bring together expertise from a variety of institutions e.g. church, commerce, university, etc. The consortium approach is frequently adopted in America and Britain as a way round some of the difficulties mentioned above.

The Vesper International Forum California USA: A Case Study

Vesper International Forum based at San Leandra in California USA is a typical example of a consortium. Its publicity literature states that:

'Vesper International Forum maintains an international network of individuals and organisations willing to invest expertise, time and resources, in order to develop partnerships among political, academic, business, labor and religious organisations. Included in the partnership for the past decade have been the German Evangelical Academies and the Hinksey Centre in England. Through these associations the Vesper International Forum identifies ethical concerns and promotes dialogue and action on social issues. This is accomplished through international, cross-disciplinary and multi-stakeholder conferences. A variety of businesses and other institutions usually attend.'

Following each conference, the Vesper Forum continues to keep in touch with the institutions which attend in order to ensure that the new perceptions and proposals discovered at each conference are publicised and implemented.

In 1990 the Vesper Society held an important international conference in San Francisco on 'Just Profits: Wending our way through the Moral Maze.'

The Reverend Chris Beales, former Secretary of the Industrial and Economic Committee of the Church of England Board of Social Responsibility, was present at that conference and describes how they tackled one of the case studies:[3]

'The Chief Executive Officer of the Dorrance Corporation has to decide, on the basis of presentations by the various divisions of the company of their operating plans and budgets for the next three years, what needs to be done in order to achieve a 13% profit growth for the next three years. There are a number of alternative proposals under consideration:

'Should a production process in Costa Rica with probable harmful effects on the environment still go ahead? Should research expenditure, a long term investment, be cut in order to assist short-term profitability goals? With a monopoly product, should the company maximise its profits (at least in the

short term) before competitors come along by charging whatever the market will bear? Should a batch of Savolene, (a new
Dorrance injectable drug for the treatment of serious viral
infections) be sold to the Philippines Government, even though
the United States Food and Drug Administration has rejected
it as being below (an extremely high) standard for the U.S.
market?'

The delegates present wrestled with these proposals in
small groups. Such conferences which discuss practical case
studies often have a very important influence upon company
policy of those who take part and can result in transforming
the business.

In 1991 the annual conference of the Vesper International
Forum was held in Pennsylvania. The subject under discussion
related to the subject matter of this book, namely lay ministry.
It is to be hoped that the conference helped to reform some of
the policies and priorities of the churches represented and
persuaded the institutional churches in America to take lay
ministry more seriously!

The Bay Area Ethics Consortium and the Centre for Ethics and Social Policy

The Bay Area Ethics Consortium is another example in California of a professionally run consortium. The Director, Bill
Maier, describes it as a joint business-academic-theological
community effort. The consortium provides training and
consultancy to companies and organisations in the field of
corporate ethics.

One of the academic consultants of the Consortium is
Professor Charles McCoy. He believes that an important
method of transforming policies within institutions is through
what he calls the 'triadic approach'. This brings the combined
insights of those who specialise in theology and ethics and the
social sciences together with policy makers in the chosen
institution. When I met Professor McCoy he stressed the
importance of the Church working alongside the social
scientists and policy makers as an 'inter-active social' group.

He said, 'We work with organisations, particularly business organisations, at their request. We negotiate the details,
e.g. confidentiality, length of project (it must not be a "quick

fix"), and we always get the Chief Executive to make the formal announcement that it will happen. Each person in the company who is involved in the project is interviewed by the theological/ethical consultant and the social science consultant. From these interviews a "company values profile" is built up. This is then fed back and checked out to 'make sure that we have heard correctly". This is then described as the company corporate ethic.

The next stage involves probing further in order to ascertain whether the corporate ethic is realistic or merely aspirational. How do intentions and actuality cohere? How can the policy be implemented?

After this, it is necessary to wean the company away from the consultants so that everyone in the company can own the new policy. This process not only ensures that people are aware of what they are doing, but also communicates the philosophy. This is not the same as a promulgation of a code of ethics.'

McCoy mentioned, in the interview he gave me, several companies, which as a result of this triadic consultative approach had changed their corporate ethical policies. The Wells Fargo Bank, for example, had before the consultancy, concentrated their business in safe middle class 'white' areas. After the consultancy they changed their policy and opened several branches in 'black' and 'hispanic' areas which became highly profitable.

Managing Values

Charles McCoy, who is also associated with the Bay Ethics Consortium, is the author of a book entitled *Managing Values*. He maintains that the 'bottom line' should never become the ultimate measure of company performance. He points out that even Friedman, (who taught that 'the social responsibility of business is to increase its profits'), admitted that the 'bottom line' is never the only measure of performance. Other values, e.g. short-term gains versus long-term gains, have to be taken into consideration.

McCoy says that the art of management requires evaluating alternative priorities. Because management involves the 'weighing alternative values', it is impossible to avoid business ethics. The Company Corporate Ethic is at the heart of management. Ethics and performance are closely related.

'The real choice facing managers', says McCoy, 'Is whether they "fly blind" or are clear about the way they set priorities and choose the values that control corporate policy. They need to manage values as carefully as they manage financial affairs. Projections about the social consequences can be as risky and as wrong as financial predictions. Managers must also be sensitive to the changing values of society around them.'

The American Motor Industry is a classic example of a failure by management to perceive customers' changing values. In 1950 the USA built 80% of all cars in the world. By 1981 the percentage dropped below 30%. By 1991 it had dropped much further. An important factor in this decline is that the management of Ford, General Motors and Chrysler made corporate policy decisions in isolation from changing customer needs. The oil crisis of the 1970s led customers to require small, fuel efficient, environmentally friendly cars, but the American manufacturers were still building big, thirsty vehicles and encouraging their customers to remain loyal to the traditional American car industry. They misjudged the ethical climate.

In this chapter we have so far explored ways in which people live and work within institutions. We have noted how institutions tend to have a life of their own and can exert a powerful influence (for good or ill) over the people who operate within them. Institutions may transmit values into the wider community. Commercial companies, for example, may encourage consumerism values. We have seen also how institutions can compete with one another and even seek to destroy one another.

For these kinds of reasons people within institutions need support. In this book we are thinking in particular about the ways in which Christian lay people can be supported by the Church in their day-to-day secular ministries within institutions.

However, as we have seen, it is no use supporting individuals within institutions unless the Church also makes some attempt to transform the institutions themselves and seeks to reform their corporate ethic where necessary.

The Church's Industrial Mission has been greatly helped

in recent years by the adoption by many companies of the word 'mission'! Nowadays many companies have 'mission statements' which set out the corporate objectives and strategy of the company. Thus, for example, the Mission Statement of British Telecom reads:

'British Telecom's mission is to provide world class communications and information products and services and to develop and exploit our networks at home and overseas.'

One starting point in the process of transforming institutions is the introduction of a corporate ethic into the company mission statement.

Professor Charles McCoy of the Bay Area Ethics Consortium in America identifies three perspectives in developing a corporate ethic within an institution:

Firstly there is what he calls the ethic of corporate self interest, secondly the ethic of multiple responsibility and thirdly the ethic of social vision.

Self Interest

This is the most basic ethical perspective and concerns the survival of the institution, its profitability and its success. John Wesley enunciated this ethic succinctly when he gave this advice:

'Gain all you can, save all you can, give all you can.' This may lead to 'laissez-faire' economics, and so self-interest needs to be broadened and related to other ethical perspectives.

The Ethics of Multiple Responsibility

The ethics of multiple responsibility has evolved from the realisation that institutions are inter-dependent one with another. No institution is an island. It affects a multiplicity of other institutions and groups such as customers, shareholders, elderly people, young people, and the wider community. There is an ever-widening circle of groups to whom responsibility must be recognised.

Social Vision

Thirdly, there is the ethic of social vision. A vision for the future. This vision must take into account the goals of other organisations, other sections of society and the diverse views of 'the good society'.

A comprehensive ethic combines and reconciles the three ethical perspectives outlined above and these ethical policies can be incorporated into the process of formulating other aspects of company policy, e.g. a bank's loan policy, redundancy policy and the management of change.

Industrial Mission

Like the consortia in America, for many years Industrial Mission in Britain has sponsored conferences and training programmes in an attempt to influence corporate values and company policies. The format of Industrial Mission conferences always includes some kind of theological or ethical reflection.

In the early 1960s the Croydon Industrial Mission organised a major conference on the theme 'Managing Change'. I was Senior Industrial Chaplain in Croydon at the time and I remember that the conference was well attended. One company, Louis Newmark Ltd, was represented at the conference by the Managing Director, the Personnel Manager and the Trade Union Convener. Some years later I met the Managing Director.

'Do you remember that conference you organised on "Managing Change"?' he asked. 'Well, at that time we were contemplating a number of important changes in our company and as a result of attending your conference we managed those changes very differently from our original plans and I want to thank you.' That conversation has always given me great encouragement.

More recently, in March 1991, the Churches' Industrial Group Birmingham, in conjunction with the Rotary Club of Birmingham, the British Institute of Management, the Institute of Business Ethics and a number of other organisations, arranged a one day conference on Business Ethics entitled GOOD BUSINESS. The conference included three addresses by senior managers from three key sectors of industry in the West Midlands: Cadbury Ltd, the Rover Group and Barclays Bank plc.

All three companies described how they sought to apply ethical principles in practical terms in their corporate policies.

Mr F. D. Brooks the Managing Director of Cadbury's referring to a comment made by Sir Adrian Cadbury when he was Chairman of Cadbury Schweppes plc, said:

We are *Cadbury* - the first name in chocolate

Cadbury Means Quality .... this is our promise. Our reputation is built upon Quality; our commitment to continuous improvement will ensure that our promise is delivered.

In supplying chocolate products that provide enjoyment, satisfaction and value to our consumers.

In working closely with all our customers and our other business partners to achieve mutual success.

In achieving levels of profitability and growth which provide a proper return on our shareholders' investment, and encourage continuing investment in the business.

In creating an environment that welcomes the challenge of change, and encourages the contribution of every one of us to achieve both personal fulfilment and business success.

In being a socially responsible business and good neighbour in the communities in which we operate.

In acting with fairness and integrity in all our dealings.

F. DAVID BROOKS
MANAGING DIRECTOR

'There is no conflict between the values and characteristics we have inherited from the past and the action we now need to take to ensure a successful future for the company.'

He outlined the company mission statement: [4]

'Cadbury means quality . . . our commitment to continuous improvements will ensure our promise is delivered.

In supplying chocolate products that provide enjoyment, satisfaction and value to our customers.

In creating an environment that welcomes the challenge of change, and encourages the contribution of every one of us to achieve both personal fulfilment and business success.

In being a socially responsible business and good neighbour in the communities in which we operate.

In acting with fairness and integrity in all our dealings.'

Mr Roger Twiney for the Rover Group described Rover's corporate ethics. 'Starting from a need to be competitive and legally compliant the Company has moved to "institutionalise" environmental awareness into its decision-making process.'

Mr J. T. T. Hindley from Barclays Bank described how the need to make profits has to be set alongside ethical considerations and other corporate objectives such as staff career development and company responsibility to the community.

Another senior manager outlined the Co-operative Bank's code of practice which sets out ethical criteria to be used in investment policy.[5] The code includes the following statements:

'We will not loan, invest or supply financial services to countries governed by oppressive regimes.

We will not help finance companies that manufacture and export arms and weapons to countries that oppress people.

We will not supply any person or company that causes animal suffering through intensive factory farming.'

The Churches' Industrial Group Birmingham received encouraging reports from organisations represented at that Business Ethics conference. A practical result has been the establishment of a Centre for Business Ethics in the heart of the city.

In closing this chapter it is worth noting the excellent work which has been done for a number of years at St George's House, Windsor Castle. This is a Christian foundation. Here, top level consultations are held, bringing together

The Co-operative Bank Ethical Policy.

"Can a bank exert a positive influence on the future of the World? Can you? Together we can at least try. We can stand up and let our views be known. We can show that behaviour that is unacceptable to society should not be acceptable in business. We can act as a force for a change."

2 Terry Thomas, MD Co-operative Bank.

1. **We will not** loan, invest or supply financial services to countries governed by oppressive regimes.

2. **We will not** help finance companies that manufacture and export arms and weapons to countries that oppress their people.

3. **We will not** invest in any business involved in testing cosmetics on animals.

4. **We will not** support any person or company that causes animal suffering through intensive factory farming.

5. **We will not** offer financial support to a business, farm or other organisation engaged in the production of animal fur.

6. **We will not** support any organisation involved in blood sports.

7. **We will not** invest in or loan to manufacturers of tobacco products.

8. **We will** try to ensure that none of our services are exploited for the purposes of money laundering, drug trafficking or tax evasion.

9. **We will** help and encourage all our business customers to adopt a pro-active stance on the environmental impact of their own activities.

10. **We will** actively seek out individuals, commercial enterprises and non-commercial organisations that have a complementary ethical attitude.

11. **We will** extend and strengthen our Customer Charter in order to maintain our high standards of customer confidentiality.

12. **We will** continuously re-appraise our customers' views on all of these and other issues and develop our ethical stance accordingly.

The COOPERATIVE BANK

senior people in business, the professions, trade unions, the churches, government, etc. The influence of these conferences, at which members of the Royal Household sometimes attend, is very far reaching indeed. These high level consultations have a profound impact upon the reformation of policies and the transformation of institutions.

Finally, it should not be forgotten that shareholders of companies can exert considerable influence upon company policy. A lobby of shareholders can sometimes work marvels in transforming institutional practice. This can be one of the most effective ways to minister in the market place.

CHAPTER TEN

Reciprocal Counselling

Some problems which people encounter 'at the front line' are purely technical and cerebral. However, human beings are not computers. They have a heart as well as a mind. (They also have a soul, but that is the subject of the next chapter!) There is invariably an emotional element in dealing with problems and people at the front line.

Whereas people in other parts of the world feel completely free to express their emotions, a display of emotion would appear to be out of place, and not the 'done thing' in the 'best' British society.

At the time that I was trained at an Anglican theological college (in the 1950s) a display of emotion by ordained ministers was even regarded as out of place in the Church of England! Clergy were trained to be straight-faced and controlled at all times.

The result of this Anglican training is that most clergy of my generation still hide their emotions from public view and sometimes cannot even discharge their emotions privately. Clergy are often the most difficult people to counsel because, though they can discuss problems in a cerebral way, they will not 'let go' of their emotional distress.

This problem is part of the British culture. Whereas babies and young children cry quite naturally when hurt, the British adult faces pain bravely. It is definitely not British to cry 'at the front line' however painful the pressures which build up! The result of this 'bottling up' of emotional stress is that when a breakdown does occur it is likely to be dramatic.

It is increasingly recognised that it is very important to release emotional stress as part of the natural bodily function. It is not crude to say that just as it is natural and important to open bowels regularly so it is natural and important to 'excrete' emotional stress regularly. Such 'excretion' (though perhaps, like the opening of bowels, best done in private!) is not something shameful, unnatural or a sign of weakness. On the contrary it is all part of sensible healthy living.

The Church's support for people at the front line ought to include the safe place for this 'discharge' to take place. Sometimes it will be suitably trained clergy themselves who offer expert support to enable people to discharge their emotional stress. Sometimes clergy may recommend the 'professional' support of a trained counsellor.

In most 'non crisis' cases however it is better for people to help themselves. One way of doing this is in a 'safe' co-counselling group. These groups often meet on a monthly basis in order to facilitate reciprocal counselling. An organisation known as Co-Counselling International provides this facility. Co-counselling groups can be found in most towns and cities in Britain.

What is Co-Counselling?

Co-counselling is a method of self development. It is not a Church-based organisation though many Christians take part in co-counselling groups.[1]

Put simply, co-counselling enables two people to come together to give each other reciprocal support. First one is client and the other is counsellor and later the roles are reversed. The time available is shared equally between them.

Before joining a co-counselling group, prospective members are asked to take a course of fundamental training. This training is considered to be absolutely essential and filters out those people who are not capable of offering to another person the kind of detached 'attention' that clients need. Their own emotional 'stuff' may be such as to prevent them listening with due sensitivity to the other person. If a person has so much distress that he or she cannot give required attention to a co-counselling partner, alternative methods of counselling are suggested. It is important that such people are referred to appropriate alternative counselling support and are not left feeling rejected. Having said that, it must also be said that co-counselling is not for everybody. It is only for those people who are capable of reciprocal counselling. This means firstly, as counsellor, an ability to give complete attention to another person, and secondly, as client, an ability to use a counsellor as a 'tool' with the same kind of objectivity as any other kind of tool is used, in this case in order to be able to discharge pent-up hurtful emotion, or to celebrate and affirm skills and success.

For this reason a characteristic of all co-counselling is that the client is always in control. Co-counselling is always 'client centred'. A 'contract' is established between client and counsellor at the beginning of each session so that the client can determine the kind of 'intervention' (if any) that he or she wants from the counsellor. This may vary from asking the counsellor to listen without comment, to more frequent intervention in order to assist when the client appears to be evading sensitive material. But it is for the client to request the type of contract that he or she wants. It goes without saying that confidentiality is absolutely essential at all times. No counsellor will mention a person's material, either to another person or to the client, outside a counselling session. After frequent counselling a client's material is quickly forgotten anyway, and in no way is there any embarrassment when meeting afterwards in a social context.

There are other basic ground rules which are explained to people when they join the co-counselling community. No harassment is an obvious example.

In most localities co-counselling groups consist of up to a dozen people. They may meet as a group on a regular basis, e.g. once a month. These monthly meetings help people to develop various skills, take part in workshops for further training, and enable people to find appropriate partners for regular co-counselling sessions in between the monthly meetings.

All this may appear at first to be frightening to an outsider! However, in my experience all the co-counselling groups that I have been associated with are warm and very supportive. I have been a member of the co-counselling community for over a decade. I have experienced many other types of support groups such as 'T' (for Training) groups which were very popular in the 1970s. The idea behind such groups was to remove tasks in order to concentrate on individual and group needs but they were frequently cold and forbidding! Among the many types of counselling groups for people 'at the front line', co-counselling is the one 'general purpose' group that I would recommend for most people.

Fundamental Training for Co-counselling

A 'fundamentals' course in co-counselling usually lasts for a minimum of 40 hours. Courses are available in many colleges or from local communities by arrangement. Courses may be specially arranged for church groups.

During the 'fundamentals' course, people learn to be both clients and counsellors. They are introduced to a variety of simple techniques to use with each other that enables them to release stored-up distress. The results are that people become more energetic and develop a more celebratory attitude towards themselves and towards those around them.

This is not intended to be a text book of co-counselling but by way of illustration I mention here a few of the techniques which are offered during training.

The first essential for a counsellor to learn is the ability to listen and to distinguish 'counselling' from 'conversation'. In particular the counsellor learns to listen to the feelings which may lie behind the words used by the client. The counsellor's task is to help the client express feelings and 'discharge' these feeling in a safe way – by crying, laughing, shouting, banging a pillow or whatever way may be safely appropriate.

It is not the job of the counsellor to give advice or to be judgemental. The counsellor's role is to 'be there' for the client as he or she works at his or her 'stuff'! Appropriate interventions may, however be helpful. Often simply picking up the last word or phrase used by the client may be sufficient to keep the client 'talking' if the client gets 'stuck'.

Eye contact at all times is useful, but not essential. Evasion of eye contact may indicate possible evasion in other ways. A pillow or cushion and a plentiful supply of paper tissues are useful! The cushion can be used as an object for the client to talk to or even hit if necessary! People at the front line frequently have all kinds of feelings about their superiors and subordinates and it is helpful for clients to be enabled to 'act out' these feelings. A simple technique for the counsellor to use is a phrase like: 'What would you like to say to your boss . . .?' or even

'What would you like to do to him or her . . .???!!'

If a client is on the point of discharging anger or grief, the counsellor's task is to assist this to happen, offering the cushion to be cried into or hit as appropriate. The discharge of tension can sometimes be assisted by appropriate bodily contact. Often simply rubbing the client's back may relieve tension or offering the cushion to 'push' against when a client wishes to work at feelings of being smothered or 'put upon'. Embraces should not be considered at all out of place when requested by the client. The need to feel loved and wanted is very important.

These and other techniques, such as validation, mimicry, assisting clients to re-live past experiences and 'guided fantasy' are usually taught in the basic 'fundamentals' course. More specific training in dealing with emotions such as anger, grief, guilt, sexuality, isolation, etc. is also included in the course.

At the end of each co-counselling session (which may last for about thirty minutes) it is important for the counsellor to make sure that the client is back in 'present time'. This can be done by setting clients a few simple tasks such as spelling their name backwards!

It is as important to receive training on how to be a client as it is on how to counsel. The client is always in control. The counsellor is there as a tool to enable the client to discharge stress. The first step is to build up mutual trust. Simple 'trust games' can be used for this purpose. People can take turns to be in the middle of a circle and fall backwards in a relaxed way into the supporting arms of the group. A similar exercise can be used by people in pairs. The client will ask his or her counsellor to let him or her fall backwards before being supported. The client may begin by asking perhaps for three inches, then six inches, then one foot and (as confidence is built up), three feet, or even eight feet and so on. The client always sets the limit that he or she can trust the counsellor to fulfil.

In a co-counselling session, the client may make certain requests to the counsellor, e.g. to act a role in a role play exercise. An experienced client will be aware of certain techniques to use to induce emotional discharge. Yawning and deep breathing are useful techniques. It is sometimes helpful for clients to imagine themselves as children again and re-enact childhood scenes with parents, teachers and other 'authority figures'. Many people are aware of rigid unhelpful patterns in their behaviour. These patterns are caused by the accumulated hurts that we receive throughout our lives but particularly in our formative years. Co-counselling provides opportunities for these hurts to be re-examined and discharged.

Sometimes a client may know in advance how to use a thirty minute session. Something may have happened 'at the front line' in the office, factory, school (or wherever that front line is) that is painful. That will be the obvious subject to be worked on at the co-counselling session. Sometimes however it will not be obvious in advance what needs to be 'worked on'. In that case a five minute 'what's on top' exercise may be helpful. The client simply talks about feelings or experience that is on top of the mind at the present moment. By 'rambling around' in this way for five minutes the client may discover the topic that needs further work for the remaining twenty-five minutes of the session.

As well as working on hurtful experiences and rejections it is important for clients to celebrate their skills and strengths. Celebration of self is essential. Frequently our natural reticence prevents us from doing this. Sometimes Christian teaching places an undue emphasis upon self-denial, for example, giving up beer or tobacco for Lent as a way of self discipline. This can easily lead to a sense of self rejection, exaggerated sinfulness and worthlessness. Celebration of worthiness and worthwhileness – including the worthwhileness of one's daily work at the front line – is of fundamental importance. Co-counselling provides opportunity and space to celebrate SELF. Group exercises can be designed to encourage and celebrate individual self worth.

Although co-counselling is principally intended to facilitate discharge of emotional stress and emotional self development, it is up to the client to decide what he or she wants to work on at each session. The client may decide to use the allotted time to tackle a 'cerebral' task such as setting objectives and targets for a year's work or dealing with an aspect of spirituality.

For those with a faith, spirituality is the focus of daily life. Spirituality should support and affirm (rather than negate) life at the front line. So, as well as the human support of a group, a co-counselling partner, or a 'mentor' we need interior support. We need to be still and know God. We need a spirituality for the front line.

CHAPTER ELEVEN

A Spirituality for the Front Line

Paradox

At first sight, the title of this chapter may appear to be a contradiction in terms. Spirituality often seems to conjure up the picture of retreat from the front line rather than spirituality at the front line. Indeed the very word 'retreat' is used as a time to come apart from the 'world' into a quiet place for spiritual reflection. Many of the great spiritual masters were people who seemed to live a life of perpetual retreat in the desert or in monasteries. The 'spiritual' and the 'worldly' seem to be 'worlds apart'.

And yet there is a paradox, for in the Jewish and Christian traditions spirituality is expected to impact upon the real world. Many of the great spiritual masters in the Old Testament, people like Isaiah and Jeremiah, were not hermits. They were people who operated in the front line of the nation's affairs and had no time for a spirituality which did not impact upon the nation's life. Take, for example, these verses from the prophet Isaiah:[1]

'What are your endless sacrifices to me? says Yahweh.
I am sick of holocausts of rams

and the fat of calves.
The blood of bulls and of goats revolts me.
When you come to present yourselves before me,
Who asked you to trample over my courts?
Bring me your worthless offerings no more,
the smoke of them fills me with disgust . . .

You may multiply your prayers,
I shall not listen.
Your hands are covered with blood,
wash, make yourselves clean.
Take your wrong doing out of my sight.
Cease to do evil.
Learn to do good,
search for justice,
help the oppressed,
be just to the orphan,
plead for the widow.'

Jesus did retreat to the wilderness on a number of occasions but He was no hermit. The spirituality which Jesus taught is a spirituality which invades and sustains every aspect of life. Like Isaiah, He had some very hard things to say about people who kept their 'spiritual life' and their 'front line' life in two separate compartments. Indeed, Jesus quotes the prophet:

'This people honour me only with lip service,
while their hearts are far from me
The worship they offer me is worthless;
the doctrines they teach are only human regulations.'
(Matthew 15 vs 8–9)

Jesus also had some hard things to say about some of the spiritual leaders of His day:
'Alas for you, Scribes and Pharisees, you hypocrites! You who pay your tithe of mint and dill and cummin and have neglected the weightier matters of the law – justice, mercy, good faith! These you should have practised, without neglecting the others. You blind guides! Straining out gnats and swallowing camels!' (Matthew 23 vs 23–24)

The Need for Affirmation

Authentic spirituality in the Christian tradition must be such as to equip people for their front line tasks. A spirituality for the front line must start from the belief that God *AFFIRMS* and approves of the work we do in our daily life, both privately and publicly. If what we do at the front line is immoral then clearly it is unrealistic to ask God to affirm us in our tasks. If our front line task involves deliberate oppression of those who are 'widows or fatherless', if it involves deliberate theft or practices which are designed to corrupt, then we invite the condemnation of Jesus: 'Alas for you . . .'

Revelations about the activities of some businesses have invited criticism about the whole process of the market economy in which many Christians work. Every activity is corruptible. Some activities may be regarded as more of a vocation than others. However the starting point is not condemnation. The starting point for a spirituality at the front line is affirmation. Our starting point is God, who loves the world so much that he gave his Son to die for the world. Our starting point is God, who seeks to affirm us in our activity. This is as true about business people as it is about priests.

Kenneth Adams, speaking at a Rotary Conference for business people in Birmingham underlined this point:

'There is no higher task to which people can devote themselves. We in business have, from time to time, to lift our eyes from our difficult but challenging daily task to see the nobility of the purpose in which we are engaged. We must affirm – deeply affirm in our hearts – the fundamental purpose of wealth creation. It is as fundamentally good as the work of the fisherman and farmer, the doctor and the nurse.'

A spirituality that supports people in economic activity must first of all affirm the essential goodness and worthwhileness of the task they perform. Kenneth Adams says:

'If the task itself is unethical, no tinkering with the rules related to that task will make it ethical. You cannot teach thieves to steal ethically!'

Affirmation and celebration is therefore an essential starting point for a spirituality at the front line. This affirmation is at the heart of the Christian Gospel of the God who loves the world so much that he gave his Son Jesus Christ to redeem and save both individuals 'one by one' and also the institutions in which people serve at the front line.

Justification

There is another dimension to a relevant spirituality at the front line. Christians believe that each individual person is justified and affirmed in God's sight, not by the success or otherwise of the work that they do at the front line, but by the fact of simply being themselves. We are justified by faith. This is important because, as we have already seen, modern society is quick to identify and value people by reason of the task they perform and the job they do. This is all right so long as they are employed. But when someone loses their job, then the cry is heard, 'Who am I?'

'I am not valued by society. I am redundant. I am "nobody".

However, in such circumstances I need to remember that in God's sight I AM still valued. I am still Me . . . Loved . . . Wanted . . . Affirmed. Supported. This is an essential element of any spirituality at the front line especially at times of economic recession.'

The Reality of Feelings

Yet although we are affirmed and valued by God, when redundancy does come and our job is lost, the feelings of loss, especially loss of identity are very deep and very real. The feelings of loss are almost parallel to the feelings of bereavement. Feelings are a reality which cannot be ignored.

'Why art thou so heavy, oh my soul, and why art thou so disquieted within me?'[2] Feelings are an important part of our humanity and should be accepted as an authentic part of any spirituality for the front line.

Let me write here from my own personal experience.

I was fortunate to be a choirboy from a very early age. So I was able, as a child, to commit many verses of scripture to memory and these passages remain a treasure trove. We sang the psalms. But there were certain verses in some of the psalms that we never sang. I could never understand why! There were brackets round them! They were considered to be 'unchristian'.

When I read them I found that they expressed feelings that I sometimes felt myself deep within. Was I wrong to have those feelings? Was I 'unchristian' to have those feelings?

In some of the bracketed verses the psalmist curses his enemies:

'Destroy them, O God; let them perish through their own imaginations: cast them out in the multitude of their ungodliness; for they have rebelled against thee.' (Psalm 5 vs 11)

'Wilt thou not slay the wicked O God: depart from me ye bloodthirsty men.' (Psalm 139 vs 19)

'We took sweet counsel together: and walked in the house of God as friends. Let death come hastily upon them, and let them go down quick into hell.' (Psalm 55 vs 15–16)

There are times when people in the front line do feel like that about colleagues, competitors, faceless managers, or sometimes even friends and loved ones. Feelings are a reality. It is no use pretending that they do not exist. We saw in the chapter which dealt with reciprocal counselling that to contain such feelings in 'brackets' is not a helpful way to deal with them. The God who 'loves the world so much' understands these feelings and accepts them. The psalmist is right to express them.

There is more to be said about this point. Sometimes we may even want to complain about God! We may feel abandoned by God. Here again the Bible is realistic about these deep feelings which can arise when things go very badly wrong. Things look black especially at times of rejection or redundancy or closure of factories, or takeovers or bankruptcy. Imagine how the staff and customers felt when BCCI closed down.

At such times when we turn to the scriptures it is tempting to jump too quickly from:

'Why art thou so heavy, O my soul, and why art thou so disquieted within me'.

to the more re-assuring,

'O put thy trust in God . . .'[3]

Yet the rejection or the feeling of abandonment and doom cannot be cured that quickly. The 'dark night of the soul' is very deep and very black. The tunnel is very long.

'The night is dark, and I am far from home'.[4]

God is like the good counsellor. He does not give us a 'quick fix'. God understands these feelings. God accepts these feelings. God encourages us to discharge these emotions in a great cry of agony and grief.

'My God, my God, why hast thou forsaken me?'[5]

The Christian believes that God's own son felt abandoned and cried out in deep agony of spirit. Jesus went through that dark night of the soul on the cross. Our faith is that Jesus goes through the dark tunnels of life alongside us whether or not we are aware of his presence with us.

The God whom we worship is the God who is with us at all times and in all places. Though at times we may feel abandoned (and the feelings are for real), God does NOT abandon us. God does not abandon us when we leave church on Sunday and start work at the front line on Monday anymore than He abandoned His own Son on the cross.

'Put thy trust in God'.[6]

Put thy trust in the God who is with us from moment to moment at the front line.

The Ever-present God

God is with us in the board room or at the trade union meeting. He is with us at the times of difficult negotiations and when we have to dismiss colleagues. He is with us as we wrestle with ethical dilemmas and as we arrive at a position of compromise. He is the ever present, ever supportive presence.

'Thou art about my path, and about my bed; and spiest out all my ways. For lo, there is not a word in my tongue: but thou, O Lord, knowest it altogether.'

'If I climb up into heaven, thou art there: if I go down to hell, thou art there also . . .' (Psalm 139 v 7)

In the midst of the hurley-burley of life at the front line we may not consciously be able to recall the reality of God's presence with us all the time, though we may have those 'momentary flashes' when we can offer 'arrow prayers' – 'God help me please to make the right decision here . . .

God may not be in the forefront of our minds but the very work that we do from moment to moment is itself prayer.

The Cistercian monks had a motto that everyone at the front line should take note of: *Laborare est orare* 'to work is

to pray. We can offer all our work to God as prayer 'that what
we do in anything to do it as for THEE'.[7]

Retreat

We are considering the components of a spirituality at the
front line. The front line can be a place of pressure and
constant stress. But God is with us at the front line, whether
we realise it or not.

However, in spite of what I said at the beginning of the
chapter, those of us who work at the front line do need
moments for reflection and prayer to realise and to internalise
God's presence. Somehow during the day, time must be found
to seek God's guidance and the power of his Spirit.

A spirituality at the front line requires time and space for
prayer and meditation each day, and occasional space for
longer periods of retreats.

It may be possible to 'snatch' moments for recollection in
the midst of the work. Coffee or tea breaks may provide a
'breathing space' though these breaks are frequently interrupted.

It is best, however, if we can give ourselves at least a
quarter of an hour each day to be quiet, without interruption
in a private space where we can relax, either alone or with
like-minded colleagues. Sometimes a city centre church may be
open early in the morning before we start work or in the
evening at the end of the day's work. Sometimes it may be
more convenient to find a 'quiet room' where it might be
possible to sit or even perhaps to lie on the floor and relax
using a variety of relaxation exercises.

The repetition of a simple 'mantra' may sometimes help
to quieten the mind and relax the body:
'Be still, and know God . . .'

Deep breathing can help in this relaxation process. We
may use the mantra 'Jesus', and breathe in on 'Je . . . ' and
breathe out on '. . . sus'.

Internal Peace

I have been impressed as an Industrial Chaplain by the number
of times that I have seen the text 'Go placidly . . .' on the desks
of busy executives.

This seems to reflect the instinctive need to be still, to be quiet, in order to have 'a right judgement in all things . . .'

'Go placidly amid the noise and haste
and remember what peace there may be in silence.
Be at peace with God, whatever you conceive Him to be,
and whatever your labours and aspirations
in the noisy confusion of life,
keep peace with your soul . . .'[8]

That last phrase is important . . . 'keep peace with your soul'.

Sometimes busy executives or professional people cannot 'keep peace with their soul' because, deep down, they cannot accept themselves. Over the course of many years as an industrial chaplain I have met busy people at the front line who have used their 'busy-ness' as a cover and defence.

Sometimes this 'busy-ness' has led to breakdown . . .not from the work itself, nor even from the stress of decision making at the front line, but because of the internal stress that is buried deep within the soul protected by 'busy-ness'.

There are many reasons why people cannot 'keep peace' with their soul. Sometimes the causes are either racial or sexual.

There is a great deal of racial discrimination at the front line. In spite of legislation there are all sorts of subtle ways of discrimination which cause hurt particularly to people of ethnic minorities. This discrimination is even experienced by people in the life of the institutional church. This can cause people to feel undervalued and may lead to distress and depression. Alternatively discrimination may lead to hyper-activity, restlessness and political lobbying.

For similar reasons women may feel undervalued. The highest positions in the civil service seem to be reserved for men. Women are still under-represented in the senior ranks of British management, though the Prime Minister has recently launched a campaign to alter this state of affairs.

The questions surrounding sexual orientation are particularly topical because of the added issues surrounding AIDS which compound homophobia. In this connection full praise should be given to Her Royal Highness the Princess of Wales for her work in helping to break down barriers of fear surrounding AIDS.

DESIDERATA

GO PLACIDLY AMID THE NOISE & HASTE, & REMEMBER WHAT PEACE THERE MAY BE IN SILENCE. AS FAR AS POSSIBLE WITHOUT surrender be on good terms with all persons. Speak your truth quietly & clearly; and listen to others, even the dull & ignorant; they too have their story. ☙ Avoid loud & aggressive persons, they are vexations to the spirit. If you compare yourself with others, you may become vain & bitter; for always there will be greater & lesser persons than yourself. Enjoy your achievements as well as your plans ☙ Keep interested in your own career, however humble; it is a real possession in the changing fortunes of time. Exercise caution in your business affairs; for the world is full of trickery. Butt let this not blind you to what virtue there is; many persons strive for high ideals; and everywhere life is full of heroism. ☙ Be yourself. Especially, do not feign affection. Neither be cynical about love; for in the face of all aridity & disenchantment it is perennial as the grass. ☙ Take kindly the counsel of the years, gracefully surrendering the things of youth. Nurture strength of spirit to shield you in sudden misfortune. But do not distress yourself with imaginings. Many fears are born of fatigue & loneliness. Beyond a wholesome discipline, be gentle with yourself. ☙ You are a child of the universe, no less than the trees & the stars; you have a right to be here. And whether or not it is clear to you, no doubt the universe is unfolding as it should. ☙ Therefore be a peace with God, whatever you conceive Him to be, and whatever your labors & aspirations, in the noisy confusion of life keep peace with your soul. ☙ With all its sham, drudgery & broken dreams, it is still a beautiful world. Be careful. Strive to be happy. ☙ ☙

FOUND IN OLD SAINT PAUL'S CHURCH, BALTIMORE! DATED 1692

All this is highly relevant to any discussion of spirituality at the front line where, in the 'noisy confusion of life men and women strive to keep peace with their souls'.

Consider, for example, the deep feelings of guilt and depression which many 'gay' people experience, particularly if they have not faced up to their sexuality. These difficulties are compounded because the institutional church itself has not faced up to this issue. Some sections of the church label all gay people 'sinners'.

A typical story is that of 'George' (that is not his real name!). He said:

'The only advice I received from my vicar was to pray and fight against the temptation. It was as if I was spending all my energy in fighting against myself. The depressions were awful. Things are much different now. I have learnt to accept myself more fully. I no longer suppress my feelings nor fight against myself. I realise that my feelings are normal for people like me. I have a tremendous sense of relief and release. I can direct my energy positively. I can live with myself.'

This is not the place to enter into a detailed discussion of this matter. Suffice it to say that 'homophobia' exists in a great many institutions (both individually and corporately) and is rationalised by some Christians who are confused about what the scriptures and Christian tradition say about homosexuality. There is, for example, a confusion in some people's minds between 'gay' relationships as such (e.g. the relationship between David and Jonathan) and a condemnation of casual sex or male rape as related in the story of Sodom and Gomorrah.

Those who suffer from discrimination need to be helped and supported in their quest to be themselves.[9]

'Be at peace with God, whatever you conceive him to be,
and whatever your labours and aspirations
in the noisy confusion of life
keep peace with your soul.'[10]

This task becomes very difficult in institutional life for a sizeable percentage of people are naturally black, naturally female or naturally 'gay'. Institutions can be intolerant and discriminatory. People do feel depressed about these matters and these feelings are very real. Any spirituality for people at the front line must take these feelings seriously, provide a support group, enable people to work through these feelings in order to come to terms with themselves, and so find peace with themselves and with God . . . just as they are. As the hymn says:

'Just as I am. . . . . . . .without one plea
But that Thy blood was shed for me . . .'[11]
and the psalm:

'. . . you, O Lord, know it all.
You made me. You keep me in your care:
Your arms are continually around me.
It is good to know that, and to have the
assurance of your continual presence'. (Psalm 139)

Guilt-free Cult

Some time ago a group of Industrial Chaplains organised a workshop to discuss authentic spirituality. We discussed the kind of taboos and guilt feelings mentioned above. I was a member of that group. We realised that Christianity, in its beginnings, was essentially a movement of liberation. Other religions demanded that God (or gods) should be placated with sacrifices and religious acts. Christianity, in contrast offered a sense of 'liberation' from slavery.

This sense of liberation needs to be realised anew in our generation and in each and every age. Yet the Church sometimes clutters up our new-found freedom with taboos and restrictive practices. The Church which began as a revolution to gain freedom for humankind has become institutionalised and the institution has taken over the revolution! The Church has sometimes suggested inappropriate rules of life for lay people which have involved more and more 'cultic acts'. In the Roman Catholic Church, for example, the rules of Sunday Mass, confession and daily prayer frequently induce feelings of guilt. All churches seem to be imposing more and more demands upon their members which induce guilt if not performed.

A new realisation is required of what Christianity is all about. Jesus Christ frees us from slavery to both internal and external shackles. Whatever else it is, a spirituality for the front line is essentially a guilt-free cult. Freed from 'spiritual shackles' (and slavery to the Church) we can be empowered to perform our front line tasks and so 'live and work' to the glory of God.

CHAPTER TWELVE

A Theology for the Front Line

Sir Harold Wilson, the former Prime Minister, used the word 'theology' when he wanted to dismiss something as irrelevant. He would say 'That's just theology!' Wilson was proud of his reputation for being concerned with practical, down-to-earth matters. He despised irrelevant theory or worse still, what he called 'theology'. For him, theology meant the kind of speculation which is not earthed in reality. 'Theologians' in Wilson's meaning of the word, lived in a cloud cuckoo land!

Well, of course, there are some professional theologians in our universities and theological colleges who may indeed come within the category scorned by Wilson. They pursue their studies in a rarified academic world, inoculated from the world inhabited by 'ordinary' people. It could be argued that one of the reasons why the Church (particularly the Church of England) 'cuts no ice' in the 1990s is that many of the clergy were trained by such theologians and some of our most influential Bishops, have spent a considerable proportion of their ministry in this kind of enclosed academic environment before becoming Bishops. There are of course, many notable exceptions!!

In truth, for the Christian, theology is an intensely practical and relevant subject that cannot be left to 'ivory tower' theologians. It is especially relevant for those people who are engaged (as Wilson was!) 'at the front line'. It is not possible to do justice to the wide-ranging implications of theology for those who work in public life (or have been made redundant from their employment) in one chapter of a general book. I hope that it might be possible in this chapter at least to sketch out some important headlines which can be followed up in further study. What I am seeking to do here is provide basic theological equipment to arm those who operate on the front line in secular life. I shall examine some key theological words and key theological themes to see how they relate to real life 'front line' situations.

What is Theology?

Theology is about life and life's values – set in the context of that which is of ultimate value, whom we call God. Theology is about humankind – the relationship that humans have with each other, their relationship with the created universe and their relationship with the Creator God. Theology is concerned with human nature – what makes human beings 'whole' and 'healthy' (both as individuals and corporately) and what makes humankind less than 'whole' a state which Christian theologians call 'sin'. Moreover, Christian theology claims to have a remedy for sin in the person and work of Jesus Christ. This is the core of the Christian Gospel – the 'Good News'.

Love

Christian theology stresses the importance of love. 'It's love that makes the world go round.' By love in this sense we mean taking everyone's interest seriously, both individually and corporately. We mean also taking the interest of the whole created universe seriously. Jesus illustrated this kind of love when he told stories such as the father's love for a 'prodigal' son; and the love that the Samaritan had for the wounded man lying by the wayside. Unlike Cain, Jesus taught that human beings have a duty to be 'their brother's keeper'. This is as true for society as it is for individuals. That is why social values are important. There is an African proverb which says: 'If the foot gets a thorn in it, the whole body must stoop down to pull it out'. We are to love our neighbours as ourselves. It implies, as we have already seen, that we must love ourselves also!

Christian theology makes further assertions. Love not only makes the world go around but Love created the world in the beginning, Love sustains the world in existence now from moment to moment and Love invites humankind to share in this ongoing activity. Love is at the very centre of the universe. Love is of God. God is Love. Moreover Love 'came down' in the person of Jesus Christ to redeem and recreate at a crucial turning point in human history and Love lives on, in and around us and invites continuing human response. This is spelt out in the pages of the Bible.

Created in the Image of God . . .

'God said let us make human beings in our own image, after our likeness, to have dominion over the fish in the sea, the birds in the air, the cattle, all wild animals on land and everything that creeps on earth.

God created human beings in his own image;
in the image of God he created them;
male and female he created them.
and God saw all he had made and it was very good.'

(Genesis 1, The Revised English Bible).

This is not fantasy. It is shot through with practical implications. Humankind is created in the image of the creator God. That is the key to human nature. God is creator. Humankind, created in God's image is created to be creative. Deprived by social circumstances (or other reasons) of the ability to be creative, a person is less human. This insight into human nature, the basic need that human beings have for creativity is of immense practical importance. Human deprivation does not merely consist of material deprivation. To be fully human is to have the opportunity to be creative. To be deprived of opportunity to express creativity is to be deprived of a basic human right. What is true of people as individuals is true also of people in groups and nations. This insight explains why human behaviour can become 'deranged' when people lack opportunity for creative fulfilment. Motor car companies in the strike prone 1970s realised this and enlightened companies looked for ways in which jobs could be made more fulfilling by using job enrichment programmes.

Work

The theological insight that humankind is created in the image of the creator God has other implications. God is a worker! God works. The book of Genesis depicts God working at His task of creation for six days. Human beings also, created in God's image are by nature workers. Work is a creative activity. This insight too has practical implications for those whose work is boring, uncreative or does not utilise their full human potential. This theological insight also has implications for those who, through unemployment are unable to work. Pope John Paul said in his encyclical, 'On Human Work', (*Laborem Exercens*) that work is a fundamental dimension of Man's existence on earth. To be deprived of work is to be deprived of a fundamental part of our full humanity. Archbishop William Temple said a long time ago that unemployment is a corrosive poison. It saps both physical and moral strength. The worst effect of unemployment is not the physical event but the moral disaster.[1]

Stewardship

The Bible also speaks of Man's 'dominion'. This is a misleading interpretation. A better translation is the word 'stewardship'. As 'co-creator' and 'co-worker' with God, the Bible teaches that human beings have been given stewardship over the created universe.

'The Lord God took Man and put him in the garden to till it and keep it', (Genesis 2 verse 15).

This has wide implications for the management and conservation of resources. Environmental issues are also implicated.

Labour

However, as well as being given stewardship over the created universe, human beings share many of the characteristics of the animal kingdom especially the need to labour: 'Man goeth forth to his work and to his labour until evening.' (Psalm 104 vs 23).

Hannah Arendt, in her book entitled *The Human Condition*[2] draws attention to the important distinction between labour and work. Whilst human beings share with God the creative capacity to work to produce things. Human beings also share with animals the need to labour in order to survive.

Hannah Arendt points out that every European language, both ancient and modern, contains two etymologically unrelated words (labour and work) for what is sometimes thought to be the same activity. But there is an important distinction between these two words. Human beings are both 'Animal Laborans' and 'Homo Faber'. Labour is a term which has long been used in British industry to describe employees who undertake certain types of jobs. In any group of managers the 'high cost of labour' (compared with what is still available in some parts of the world) is a frequent topic of conversation.

The ancient Greeks distinguished craftsmen who produced 'work' from 'slaves' 'who like animals with their bodies minister to the necessities of life'. (Aristotle Politics 1254 b25). The philosopher Locke also drew attention to this distinction: 'the labour of our bodies and the work of our hands'.

Following Locke, Hannah Arendt defines labour as 'the activity which corresponds to the biological process of the human body, – growth, metabolism and eventual decay'.[3] Labour is that activity which ensures the survival and continued life of the species. This is in line with the thought of Karl Marx who defined labour as 'man's metabolism with nature'.

Labour signifies pain and effort and the word is also used for the pangs of child-birth. Labour is derived from the latin word *laborare* which means to stumble under a burden. The word 'labour' therefore refers to the effort involved in muscular activity such as pushing, pulling and heaving.

The reader may be forgiven at this point for thinking that perhaps Harold Wilson may have been correct in his assessment of theology and that I may be in danger of taking off into the stratosphere in pursuing this line of thought. But no! Here again there are very practical implications especially for those who 'labour at the front line'. Four such implications are outlined briefly here:

1. The dignity of human nature

2. The rhythmic nature of labour

3. The solidarity of labour

4. The redemption of labour

The Dignity of Human Labour

The ancient Greeks had a contempt for labour. Slaves (like women in travail) were 'hidden away' from society. Slaves had no place in public life. In contrast the Christian tradition takes the opposite view. Those who labour are affirmed. In one of the very earliest Christian letters (that of St Paul to Philemon) the high estate of slaves is commended.

Biblical thought, in contrast to Greek thought, does not consider labour degrading. On the contrary, the Bible sees labour as part and parcel of man's very nature . . . part of his essence of being human.

The Rhythmic Nature of Labour

Arendt says: 'The joy of labour is the human way to experience the sheer bliss of being alive which we share with all living creatures. To labour is the only way human beings can remain and swing contentedly in nature's prescribed cycle – toiling and resting, labouring and consuming, with the same happy regularity with which day and night, life and death follow each other.'[4]

The seven dwarfs in Walt Disney film 'Snow White' rejoiced to sing:

> 'Hi ho, hi ho,
> It's off to work we go
> We keep on singing all day long
> Hi ho, hi ho.'

They sang, not because they produced any great 'work' but because:

> 'We dig dig dig dig
> dig dig dig
> We dig the whole day through . . . '

Rhythm is an important insight. Labour is best performed rhythmically. Hence there are 'labour songs'. It is not without significance that 'canned' music is frequently provided in factories in the belief that it improves productivity.

The Solidarity of Labour

Labour solidarity is an important bond which has not been completely severed even by Mrs Thatcher during her years in office! Nor has the collapse of communism in Eastern Europe diminished the important experience of human beings labouring together. The biological rhythm of labour unites a group of labourers to the point where each member of the team may feel that he or she is no longer an individual but actively one with other comrades. This comradeship eases 'labour's toil and trouble' in much the same way as soldiers marching together in a squad eases the effort of walking long distances with heavy burdens. Labour 'solidarity' has been an important factor in human history over many years.

The Redemption of Labour

Labour was originally intended by God to be good and a source of great rejoicing. In human history labour has often become hard toil and full of sorrow as a result of human sin. (Genesis 3 v 17) We can think, for example, of the abuse of child labour by the Victorians and in present times by businesses in the Far East.

Alan Richardson in his *Theological Word Book* says:[5]

'The world of labour is disarranged as a consequence of human sin. The Biblical myth implies that all drudgery, bitterness and wretchedness of man's workaday life is the consequence of his rebellion against God.'

But redemption is always a possibility.

In the Bible, great significance is attached to the story of the deliverance of the Children of Israel from their slavery in Egypt. They lived a life of misery, sweating and toiling under the harsh hands of the Pharoah. Deliverance seemed impossible. Yet, led by Moses, the impossible happened. That redemption experience made a profound impression upon the Children of Israel ever afterwards: 'We were slaves in Egypt and the Lord brought us out of Egypt with a mighty hand.'[6]

The hand of God was seen to be at work in this act of salvation and this important historical event is seen by Christian theologians to be the 'prototype' of mankind's deliverance from bondage to sin bought by Jesus Christ. This is the Good news of the Christian Gospel as set out in the well known Easter hymn:

'Come ye faithful, raise the strain
Of triumphant gladness!
God hath brought his Israel
Into joy from sadness;

Loosed from Pharoah's bitter yoke
Jacob's sons and daughters
Led them with unmoistened foot
Through the Red Sea waters.

'tis the spring of souls today
Christ hath burst his prison
And from three days' sleep in death
As a sun has risen;
All the winter of our sins,
Long and dark, is flying
From his light, to whom we give
Laud and praise undying.'[7]

Alan Richardson says that it is significant that Jesus, when he came to redeem mankind, should have been born into an ordinary working class family, (John 5 v 17) and that 'he took the form of a slave' (Phillipians 2 v 7). Jesus assumed servitude to save mankind from servitude.

Redemption is costly. Redemption is an economic word. Redemption cost Jesus Christ his life. He bore the pain and suffering of it all, refusing to be 'anaesthetised' by drugged wine. As we look around the world today and survey the lot of humankind, particularly in Eastern Europe, we know that the redemption of human labour is still a costly process. There has to be a death to old ways of doing and to old ways of thinking. That may involve a drastic reshaping of industry and rethinking old attitudes to labour. Some would seek salvation in automation. Great riches can be derived with little human effort using sophisticated technology. Automation provides us with an opportunity to 'anaesthetise' labour. Yet, as Hannah Arendt points out,[8] that whilst the longing to be free from labour is as old as history, humankind cannot really experience *true free-*

dom unless it always remembers that it is possible to be subject to necessity. Happiness can only be achieved where life's processes of exhaustion and regeneration, pain and relief from pain, labour and rest strike a perfect balance. Arendt concludes that the fulfilment of that long felt wish to be liberated from labour has come at a moment when it could be self-defeating.

'It is a society of labourers which is about to be liberated from the fetters of labour (i.e. by automation) and this society no longer knows of those other higher and more meaningful activities for the sake of which this freedom would deserve to be won.'[9]

So it may follow that Christians in the front line of industrial life should look for signs of Christ's redeeming activity, not in the anaesthetics of automation but in opportunities for labour and work which provide human fulfilment balanced by 'rest' in the Biblical sense of that word.

Rest

We have already spoken about the need for a balance between labour and rest in the chapter on stress and the chapter on spirituality. We saw in those chapters how modern society is in danger of getting the balance wrong. In the Ten Commandments, labour and work are set in the context of Sabbath rest.

The concept of 'rest' in the Bible is as important as the concept of labour. Mankind's natural need, which is shared with the animals, is to expend energy, feel exhausted and then rest. Yet the Bible goes on to expound how 'rest' has a deeper significance for humankind than it has for the animals. We are restless till we find our true rest in God. Mankind needs to rest in order to know God: 'Be still and know God'[10]

As we saw in the last chapter, human beings need to take time to rest in order to discover God and allow themselves to be discovered by God. We need time for reflection in order to see our labour in the context of eternity. Only then can we sing with George Herbert:

> 'Forth in thy name O Lord I go
> My daily labour to pursue
> Thee, only thee resolved to know
> In all I think or speak or do'.[11]

Leisure

We have been examining a number of words and theological themes that have some relevance to people who are involved in the 'front line' of secular life. We have noted the distinction between 'work' and 'labour'. We have seen that it is possible to both go to work and to labour without necessarily being employed to do so. We have spoken also about 'creativity' and 'rest'. Now we explore another word – leisure.

The leisured way of life was very important for the ancient Greeks. The Greeks despised labour and did not hold work in very high esteem either! To the ancient Greeks even craftwork failed to possess sufficient dignity to constitute an authentic way of life.

P. D. Anthony in his book *The Ideology of Work*[12] says:

'For the ancient Greeks, all work seems to have been regarded in the same light: doctors and sculptors and schoolmasters were all paid like masons and joiners at the customary standard rate'. For Aristotle the aim of the state was to produce leisured gentlemen.

The situation was very much the same in medieval England. Hard work, though necessary for some people was not regarded as morally necessary. Max Weber in his book, *The Protestant Work Ethic and the Spirit of Capitalism*, written in 1967, describes the life of a medieval merchant:

'He led a comfortable existence, he worked from five to six hours a day, his earnings were moderately high, he had a congenial circle of friends, his life was comfortable and leisurely.'[13]

We still retain the image of the English 'gentleman' who lives a life of perpetual leisure. It has been said that the English suffer from a malaise because the average Englishman prefers to 'take his leisure at work' (i.e. during the hours that he or she is paid to be employed!) The malaise is not new. It is part of a deep seated tradition! To be fair, it must also be said that many people who work at the front line in Britain in the 1990's do so under considerable stress.

Leisure is not necessarily the same as 'rest'. Some forms of leisure involve quite hard labour! Other forms of leisure involve creative work. Many people occupy quite senior and responsible roles in the front line of public life during their 'leisure hours'. One of the fastest growing industries in Britain is the 'leisure' industry. So the word 'leisure' needs to be treated with considerable caution.

The Work Ethic – Employment and Unemployment

It was within a culture which extolled the virtue of leisure and the virtues of the 'leisured classes' that the Protestant Work Ethic emerged. The Puritans commended hard work and stressed the importance of the need to earn one's living. The link between labour and work on one hand and income on the other has been blessed with the support of scripture in a famous passage ascribed to St Paul: 'If a man will not work, neither shall he eat'. (2 Thessalonians 3 v 10).

The Protestant Work Ethic emerged at the time of the Reformation. Puritans condemned idleness. Puritans taught that a person's employment is a 'vocation' to which he or she is called by God. Business enterprise was encouraged.

The Puritans' outlook provided businesses with 'sober, conscientious and unusually industrious workmen who clung to their work as to a life willed by God'[14]. The Puritan Divine, Richard Baxter, specifically recommended the employment of godly servants. Commenting upon this, P.D. Anthony says, rather cynically: 'The engagement of God as the supreme supervisor was a most convenient device; a great part of the effort of modern management has been aimed at finding a secular but equally omnipotent equivalent in the workers' own psyche.'[15]

However, as we have already seen it is possible to work and to labour without actually being paid to do so. Therefore the so-called work ethic is perhaps more accurately defined as an employment ethic. It is now generally recognised in Britain that, with the exception of landed gentry and other 'leisured' classes, a person's income and status is linked to his or her employment. Under this arrangement society puts financial value on people by virtue of their employment and honours the individual in terms of identity and status by virtue of his or her job.

Status and identity are important words. If you ask someone who they are, they usually say, 'I'm a bricklayer . . .', 'I'm

a teacher . . .', 'I'm an engineer . . .', 'I'm a bank manager . . .'
and so on. If an unemployed person does feel a 'nobody' it can
lead to feelings of worthlessness, deep depression and even suicide.

Given a society where an increasing percentage of the
population may not, in future, be able to find employment, the
theological basis of the work/employment ethic may need re-
appraisal. In spite of St Paul's insistence on a Christian duty to
'earn' a living by 'work' it is doubtful whether there is any
authority in the Bible for a concept of 'calling' in the sense of
calling to take up a certain paid employment. The word 'call'
in the Bible usually refers to 'naming' or 'calling out'. Jesus
called people to follow him. Christians are called, not to a
particular job, but to a life of faith in Jesus Christ. We are
called, not to a work ethic, but to a life ethic of which work
(not just employment) is an important part.

Life Ethic or 'Contribution to Society' Ethic

A life ethic rather than a work ethic may therefore be a more
appropriate theology in today's technological society. This
does not imply a life of leisure but a life in which society
values and rewards a person's contribution to the community
in ways other than just through paid employment. Already
some people, for example clergy, politicians, civic dignitaries,
scout leaders, community leaders etc. are valued by the community in this way. Some of these people are not technically
employed by the community.

Anglican clergy receive stipends (not a wage or a salary)
and are inducted into 'Livings' (a significant word!). Anglican
'livings' are at present under threat as Church authorities seek
to introduce the insights of 'modern management control
systems' into ecclesiastical structures. It could, however, be a
step backwards to remove clergy freeholds or to alter the
traditional pattern whereby clergy are inducted into 'livings'
with a guaranteed income. There is much merit in giving
clergy a guaranteed income to 'be' men and women of prayer,
study and insight. Clergy need encouragement to 'be' rather
than to 'do' . . .

The question arises should everyone be entitled to a
guaranteed income whether employed or not? The principle is

already accepted that if a person is available for employment but unable to find it, he or she is entitled to receive unemployment benefit. This is, in effect, a social wage. If it becomes possible for the wealth of a community to be created by a technology which does not employ as many people as in the past, it could be expedient to devise a system whereby the wealth produced by that technology is distributed in ways other than through employment. Once people are assured of an income they can be set free to be themselves and do their creative work, physical activity and make their contribution to society in a multiplicity of ways.

Various safeguards and incentives would need to be built into this arrangement, possibly through the taxation system. This is not the place to go into details. Support would also have to be given to those who are least able to cope with free time ... but this needs to be done anyway for many of the unemployed people who wander around aimlessly today and are crying out for support.

In all this, theology is highly relevant. In applying this 'contribution to society' ethic, Christian theology, with its insights about the fallen nature of mankind, is under no illusion about the dangers and risks involved. But Christians believe that everyone has value, significance, status and dignity in God's eyes, whether they are employed or unemployed. We are all valued in God's sight, not for what we do but for who we are. We are all special in God's eyes. Christians believe in a God who has redeemed mankind's sinful ways through the death and resurrection of Jesus Christ. We are not justified by work. We are justified by grace through faith in Jesus Christ. Through Christ's death and resurrection our 'image' is recreated, our full humanity is restored. We are given new life.

> 'Lord, by the stripes which wounded Thee
> From death's dread sting Thy servants free
> That we may live, and sing to Thee
> Alleluia!'[16]

CHAPTER THIRTEEN

Unemployment

The Scope of the Problem

In the previous chapter we began to discuss unemployment. This is a topic which cannot be omitted from any consideration of ministry designed to support those who are at the 'front line'. Whether we are thinking about the problems experienced by people at the time of their redundancy, or the ongoing problems associated with unemployment, it is very much a 'front line' issue. Not least is the strain facing managers themselves who have the dreadful task of breaking the news to those people who have been declared redundant.

At the time of writing there are three million people of working age who are unemployed in Britain. These are the official figures. They are people who are registered as unemployed and who are seeking work. There are far more than three million if we include those who are not registered, those who are on training schemes and those in part-time employment on very low levels of pay. Unemployment is a growing problem. What is true of Britain is almost certainly true of Europe and most industrialised nations.

It is not just caused by world-wide economic recession, though that is a factor. It is not just a matter of tackling what economists call 'cyclical' unemployment, the cycle of booms and slumps. It is 'structural' unemployment that presents the most difficulty. There are no jobs for shepherds in big cities because there are no longer any sheep there! Even in the cities, mechanisation has increasingly taken over a lot of labouring jobs and automation has taken over other work, resulting in further 'structural' unemployment.

In Birmingham, where I live, there are very high levels of unemployment in inner city areas. In the 1980s recession, Handsworth had unemployment rates among young black people in excess of 60% I recall meeting a group of unemployed Rastafarians. There was a mood of hopelessness and utter despair. They felt that nobody seemed to care and that nothing could be done. 'Why aren't you angry?', I asked.

One of them looked at me gloomily. 'Mister, the anger has been burned out of us', he replied. It reminded me of the story that Jesus told about unemployment, 'Why are you standing about all day with nothing to do? Because no-one has hired us' (Matthew 20 v 7).

In the 1990s recession inner city areas are once again badly affected. Factories which used to employ forty or fifty people in engineering tool rooms now employ just one or two people. Computer-aided design and computer-aided manufacturing have taken over instead.

That great prophet and wit, S.J.Forrest, in a marvellous poem,[1] once suggested that even ordained ministers will be replaced by computers one day!

'Our automatic Vicar is the very latest thing,
A fine precision instrument to pray and preach and sing;
He thunders in the pulpit and he sparkles at the font,
And serves the congregation with precisely what they want'.

However, as we have already seen, there is a human tragedy in unemployment.

It is a moral and spiritual problem. In the last chapter we noted how we identify and value people by the job they do. When the job is lost people not only lose their income but they also lose their identity. Sometimes this may lead to illness, mental breakdown, marriage breakdown, crime or even suicide. This is not to say that unemployment causes these things, but if a marriage is passing through difficulties or somebody has a weak heart, the added stress of unemployment may tip them over the edge.

The Church's Role

Is there anything that the Church can do other than raise people's awareness of the difficulties surrounding unemployment and stir consciences? Certainly the former must be done because unemployment no longer seems to be an important political issue. It is no use tackling symptoms if the root cause of a disease is left untreated!

Yet practical projects are possible.

In the 1980s I was Industrial Adviser to the Bishop of Birmingham, Hugh Montefiore. Bishop Hugh set up an 'Unemployment Commission' in the Diocese of Birmingham and asked me to steer its progress.

The first thing that we did was to organise an all-night vigil with unemployed people in the Cathedral. Hundreds of unemployed people braved a bitterly cold winter's night. Bishop Hugh was there together with the Roman Catholic Archbishop and the Chairman of the Methodist District. We decided that the church dignitaries should NOT be the first to speak. We wanted, first, to enable unemployed people to tell their story. The stories were very moving and we listened and prayed. From that vigil, plans began to emerge.

The Industrial Mission set up three working parties: to see what practical advice and assistance could be given to unemployed people; to establish projects to support and retrain unemployed people; and to attempt (alongside other groups) to influence government thinking and policy. Churches throughout Britain began to set up similar working parties and at the same time a national organisation, the Church Action With The Unemployed Campaign was established.

The Bishop of Birmingham's Unemployment Commission produced a report which recommended practical ways in which local churches could give immediate support to unemployed people. We also produced a longer term strategy report entitled *Work, Employment and the Changing Future.*[2]

As a result, Industrial Mission established an organisation known as 'Inter-Church Endeavour' (ICE) to co-ordinate (ecumenically) the work of churches with unemployed people in

Birmingham. Industrial Chaplains counselled unemployed people and encouraged other ordained ministers to do so. A network of 'Drop-in' centres throughout the city was set up, staffed by unemployed people and financed under the government Community Programme. We appointed an Employment Development Officer to assist unemployed people to obtain jobs and we obtained his salary from the city council. This led to the setting up of a project known as 'Workstarter', a prototype 'Job Club'. The emphasis was upon support and to encourage unemployed people to think pro-actively rather than re-actively. This led one unemployed person to suggest that we should establish a 'sales school' to teach salesmanship and self confidence. The Employment Development Officer encouraged this idea and we managed to obtain funding for what became one of our most successful projects known as the Icebreaker Sales School. I do not pretend that all this was easy! There were difficult moments. One church member gave very generous financial support without which the project would not have been possible. Our success rate in assisting people to obtain jobs or set up businesses was very high.

Eventually, owing to further changes in government funding, we were led to establish a complete 'Managing Agency' to manage church 'Community Programmes' throughout the Diocese. The 'Head Office' of the Agency was based in one of the Birmingham city centre churches. The process of setting up the Agency involved the long and tedious task of filling in numerous forms and satisfying the detailed criteria necessary to secure funding. However, the Diocese of Birmingham provided the salary of the Chief Executive. The person appointed did an excellent job (as did all the other members of the management team) and the Managing Agency began to flourish as a 'limited liability' company.

When the government changed its programme yet again, we switched the Managing Agency so that it became an agency for training programmes. We trained unemployed people in five core skills: caring, catering, construction, clerical and computer skills. In due course the project grew too big to be housed in a city-centre church, so we decided to relocate it in a disused inner city school. All members of the management team and all the staff were recruited from the ranks of the unemployed. We were fortunate to secure a very capable board of directors which enabled the project to survive and prosper. Indeed we were able to sell the project as a successful and profitable business in a management buy-out! The project (B.C.M.A. Ltd) still exists at the time of writing (1993) and is still trading profitably.

I have described the work of the Bishop of Birmingham's Unemployment Commission and the subsequent projects in some detail in order to illustrate how it is possible for the Church to work with unemployed people and the kind of support that the church can give in this particularly sensitive part of the 'front line'. I am aware that I have used an example from the 1980s, albeit an example of an initiative that has survived into the 1990s. Government policy has changed yet again! With the establishment of local Training and Enterprise Councils ('TECs') it is no longer so easy for voluntary organisations such as churches to secure funding for ambitious projects. Nevertheless, it is still possible to do so, and 'Church Action With The Unemployed' (CAWTU) is a national charity with considerable expertise to assist local churches with initiatives.[3] There is a network of CAWTU 'contact people' throughout Britain and in addition industrial missions have a great deal of experience in working alongside unemployed people.

It would seem that unemployment is here to stay. Recessions eventually end and economies expand, yet it is doubtful if we shall ever see 'full' employment again in the industrialised nations because of changing technologies. Hence the importance of the discussion in the previous chapter about finding an alternative 'ethic' to the 'employment ethic'. I have suggested that a 'life ethic' may, in future, be more appropriate, whereby people are encouraged to make their contribution to the community in a variety of ways and receive a 'social wage'.[4] If a nation's wealth can be created by a technology which employs fewer people, alternative methods of distributing that wealth should be devised.

Many people are worried about the effects of continuing high levels of unemployment upon the fabric of society, with resulting high levels of crime, sickness, marriage-breakdowns and so on. There is a growing conviction that the time has come for another commission to be set up. This should be a high level, independent and competent national commission, consisting of people who can command the respect and confidence of all political parties. The commission should be given a very wide brief and be asked to discuss broad questions of policy both short and long term.

These issues are politically sensitive. For this reason it is all the more important that any commission should embrace the widest expertise and be free, if possible, from party political bias.

The Church should be in the vanguard of encouraging new ways of thinking about these issues given the unique insights that the Church has about the way in which God values human beings in his sight.

CHAPTER FOURTEEN

Conflict

When I first ventured into a factory as an Industrial Chaplain in 1962 the Managing Director said to me, 'We are all one big happy family here, Padre'. I soon discovered otherwise! It was not long before one shop steward came up to me and said, 'We don't want your bloody sort round here!'

I let him talk to me in this manner for some time and I then asked him what was the matter. He told me. I listened patiently. At last he calmed down. I then told him how I saw my own job. Eventually we became very good friends and over the years I was able to establish good relationships with both management and trade union representatives in this as well as other companies.

By discreet questions, I was sometimes able to ease tensions in companies that I visited and I was able to bring people together to discuss issues which were actually or potentially divisive. I remember on one occasion visiting a toolroom and hearing complaints that the managers never seem to care about the outworn machinery with which they had to cope and one man said to me, 'They have just bought new carpets for their offices!'

Some time later I was talking to a senior manager who indicated that trouble was brewing in the tool room and he did not seem to know why. I suggested that he went along to find out. He did so and the difficulties were eventually smoothed out. When visiting companies I was always very careful not to interfere with proper procedures or the proper channels of negotiation.

The 'front line' is a place of conflict.

Wherever two or three are gathered together, barriers of race, colour, class, religion, or status, etc. can sometimes be erected. Christianity is about reconciliation. Industry and commerce is an important area for the Church's Ministry of Reconciliation.

Industrial Relationships

This chapter introduces the controversial topic of Industrial Relations. Industry is one of the most powerful institutions in our society. It produces the goods and services we use. It influences working conditions, class structures, commercial pressures and moral values with profound effects on human personality and social relationships.

Deep conflicts often arise in our society through developments in new technology and world trade. Conflicts arise between those who are rich and those who are relatively poor. There are other conflicts: quality versus quantity; frustration versus fulfilment; the group versus the individual; industry versus government; concentrations of power versus the human need for participation; and management versus labour. The Church has a concern for all these matters because it is concerned with people and the institutions which influence their lives.

In spite of the diminished power of the trade unions in recent years, there are still 'two sides' of industry: those who manage and those who are managed and there are their respective representatives.

On the national scene there are EMPLOYERS' organisations such as the Confederation of British Industry, Engineering Employers' Associations, and Chambers of Commerce, and there are EMPLOYEES organisations such as large trade unions most of whom operate under the umbrella of the TUC.

In recent years there has been a considerable decline in trade union membership. Whereas in 1970 there were twelve

million people in trade unions in Britain, at the time of writing
this chapter (1993) there are only 7.7 million members. This is
mainly due to a decline in manual work, (a traditional source of
trade union membership), high levels of unemployment and
other factors such as legislation requiring trade union members
to 'sign up' every three years. In 1984, 58% of the workforce were
in trade union membership, whilst in 1990, 48% of the workforce
were members of unions. However the objectives of trade unions
remain the same as ever, namely to represent their members and
protect members' interests (particularly in collective bargaining
for wages) and improving conditions of work. From a personal
point of view the importance of trade union membership was
brought home to me very forcibly as a young child doing potato
picking during the Second World War. For a hard day's work I
was paid the sum of one shilling whilst some of my older friends
received three shillings. They protested vigorously on my behalf!

We have seen an increase in part-time work. This, coupled
with the demise of Wages Councils, has been bitterly resisted
by the trade unions who continue to campaign for full employment and for an Employees' Charter. They seek also to develop
other necessary services for their members.

In order to achieve these objectives trade unions are
continuing to merge into larger units, for example the National
Union of Railwaymen has merged with the National Union of
Seamen, the Electricians have merged with the Engineers.
Similar mergers are taking place in the service sector.

On the employers' side we have seen similar mergers
taking place. Thus the British Institute of Management has
merged with the Institute of Industrial Management. As well
as engaging in collective bargaining with trade unions, employers' organisation seek to negotiate with politicians and Government Departments on a variety of matters such as rates of
interest and taxation, etc. Sometimes employers' and employees' organisations join together in lobbies on these matters.

On matters relating to the European Community, employers' and employees' organisations have both common interests
and conflicting interests. For example trade unions are more
likely to favour the adoption of the Social Chapter, though
some employers' organisations such as the Institute of Personnel Management also favour much of the Social Chapter.

We have seen an increasing amount of legislation designed to restrict the power of trade unions coupled with a trend towards decentralised wage bargaining, and a loss of trade union recognition in many companies. It has even been stated that Britain's trade union laws infringe international conventions on human rights. Britain is now unique in Europe in not providing a legal basis for the right to strike and to stop work under dangerous conditions.[1] Former legislation, (removed by recent Conservative Governments), did at least make such important provisions. We have come a very long way since Barbara Castle proclaimed that power was on the shop floor and Prime Minister Edward Heath complained that Britain was almost ungovernable!

In the 1960s and the 1970s it was frequently said that management was unable to manage due to the power of the trade unions and thousands of days work were lost through strikes. The shop steward (as portrayed in the Peter Sellers film 'I'm All Right Jack') was a figure to be reckoned with. Yet it must also be said that most of the strikes at that time were unofficial, and more days' work were probably lost because of the common cold than were lost through strikes! Very often also, a prolonged strike was a convenient way of dealing with over production and stockpiling particularly in the motorcar industry. There has always been a certain amount of collusion between management and trade unions. Most of the shop stewards that I have met during my long experience as an Industrial Chaplain have been highly responsible people who have voluntarily taken on an unpopular job and who thereby place themselves 'in the firing line'.

The crunch came with the prolonged miners' strike, led by Arthur Scargill, when Mrs Thatcher was Prime Minister. This was a most bitter conflict. The miners were accused by the Government of holding the nation to ransom. The coal industry appeared to hold a monopoly position in energy supply, though even at that time atomic energy, oil and gas were very important in the generation of electricity. The strike led to bitter divisions within the mining communities and even within individual mining families. Eventually a 'breakaway' miners' union was formed. Mrs Thatcher was determined to crush the strike and did so, and she seemed to have public opinion on her side.

However that was not the end of the story. When, more recently, with Mr Major as Prime Minister, the President of the Board of Trade announced the sudden closure of thirty one pits, without apparent consultation there was a public outcry. The financial justification for closure (bearing in mind the huge subsidies provided for atomic-powered generating stations and the so called 'dash for gas') had been ill-prepared, and the social effects of the 125,000 jobs that would be lost together with the wider effects on community life, had not been calculated.

This raises the whole question of community life. There IS such a thing as a COMMUNITY. It is more than a collection of individuals. A community is just like a human body. If one part of the community is hurt, the whole community feels the pain. This is true whether we are dealing with a conflict situation, or with unemployment. The 'community factor' certainly came to the fore in the pit closure dispute.

At the time of the miners' strike and again at the time of the crisis over pit closures there were prominent voices within the Christian Church who spoke up for the mining communities. Some people thought that the Church should not interfere in politics, but the Church was surely right to be involved in a dispute which so deeply affected community life.

Christians in the Conflict

How far should Christians be involved in conflict and politically sensitive issues? Nowadays many companies do not have trade unions and the levels of wages and salaries are being depressed by the pressures of part-time work and the fear of unemployment. But what should be the Christian attitude towards conflict in industry? Should the Church interfere in politics? Should Christians join trade unions and accept responsibility as shop stewards? Should Christians seek to establish trade unions if none exist? And if so should Christian members of trade unions allow themselves to be brought into conflict with other Christians who are on the 'management side'? And what about the nature of jobs Christians are asked to perform?

In any 'front line' situation there is bound to be conflict sooner or later. Christians serving in the army in times of war face even more complex dilemmas. Is it right for a Christian to fight in an army where sometimes the job involves killing people? Just as in our discussion about Business Ethics we found no easy solutions (but the need for a lot of support at the front line whilst these problems were worked out), so in industrial relationships where conflict is almost inevitable, Christians on both sides need a lot of support. I believe that it is just as important for Christians to be engaged in trade union activities (and to call a strike if necessary) as it is to be engaged in managing businesses when tough decisions have to be made which may affect for good or ill the lives of many people.

Let us think a little further about the nature of the type of work that Christians may engage in. Here, too, is an area of conflict. Where is the line to be drawn? Can we affirm the production of motorcars, oil, guns, nuclear power, bombs, nuclear submarines and pornography and prostitution equally? Sometimes Christians begin to feel very uncomfortable when these matters are discussed.

To what extent is engaging in these activities part and parcel of Christian discipleship, as opposed to opportunities to offer people a chance of personal salvation by evangelism? Of course these activities may provide scope for Christian witness and Christian acts of kindness, but is engagement in secular work (either as an employer or trade union representative) 'Christian discipleship' in ITSELF? How do the values of the Kingdom square with the values of collective bargaining and industrial production to meet the conflicting demands of the market economy?

There are no easy or ready-made answers to these questions. It is not my intention to provide such answers but I would hope that such issues would be discussed in the light of Christian theological insights. Easy answers should be resisted. The temptation is either to look for a salvation purely in 'heaven above' or to adopt the solution (which evades the problem) suggested by the *Worlds Apart* report quoted in the first chapter of this book. The truth is difficult to accept but if we are to be faithful to the Biblical vision of God's purpose to bring all things together in unity, then we have to see ALL activity as 'the arena of God's purpose' including those activities which involve conflict, however bitter.

Christianity implies INCARNATION. Jesus was born into the world at a difficult point in human history and He did not avoid conflicts. The Christian task is not to avoid conflicts by taking easier options. Christians are called to be there in the secular world, stay there, and use their influence to the utmost and work through them towards a reconciling position. But in this front line activity those involved need the continual support of the Christian Church.

A 'Just' Strike

Some Christians may still not be happy at the thought of taking part in a strike so it may be worth underlining at this stage that I believe that there is such a thing as a 'just' strike. I am indebted to the late Sir Tom O'Brien MP[2] for this clear description of the characteristics of a just strike:

1. There must be a just cause.

2. All forms of negotiation must have been exhausted.

3. The good resulting from the strike must be greater than the damage caused by the strike.

4. There must be a reasonable chance of success.

5. Due consideration must be given to the harm done to innocent parties and essential services.

6. The means must be legitimate and sabotage and violence should be ruled out.

The Positive Function of Conflict . . . a Sociological Perpective

Before we examine the theological aspects of conflict it is useful to see what a sociologist has to say. Conflict, like stress, can sometimes be demonic. Yet industrial conflict does also have a positive function. Here I am grateful to Tom Lupton, a consultant in Industrial Relations. He points out that the work-place is an institution made up of people in various 'roles' such as managers, accountants, shop stewards, etc. These roles persist in time and are on-going whoever may happen to be the personalities involved at any particular time. Tom Lupton says:

'Social systems are made up of people-in-roles. The roles are linked together to form a structure which persists, whoever may happen to be the people-in-roles at a particular point in time. The structure persists because of the sets of formal rights, duties, obligations and the norms of customary behaviour which inhere in the roles and which regulate relationships between them. The stability of a particular social system is expressed by stability of expectations. Disturbances, such as disputes, anywhere in the system bring into play equilibrating mechanisms which align behaviour with expectations.'

He goes on to use the biological analogy of stability in plant life:

'Unless one defines industrial harmony, not as lack of conflict, but in terms of the effectiveness of equilibrating social mechanisms, then harmony is impossible . . . The symptoms of conflict are not evidence of the existence of disease, but as indicating the working processes in the organism which are trying to preserve the organism from internal disturbance or external pressure. Conflict therefore has positive functions.'[3]

The sociologist who looks at an industrial dispute does not normally ask who is right. He examines the effect that the behaviour he is observing has on the system in which it is taking place and asks whether the situation is likely to erupt into a temporary breakdown in co-operation or something more sinister! He concludes that conflict is the normal condition of human social organisation.

A Christian Perspective

I find myself in basic agreement with Tom Lupton as I come to the problem from a Christian perspective. Christians are bidden to love one another. But this does not mean that there should be no conflict. On the contrary love (in the sense of the New Testament Greek word agape) means taking the interests of other people seriously, at least as seriously as you take your OWN interests.

The interests of individuals and groups may, from time to time conflict, and need to be resolved. Love may co-exist with conflict. Reconciliation is the final result of conflicting interests being taken really seriously, not merely the papering over of cracks. It is certainly not Christian to pretend that 'we are all one big happy family here' when such is not the case. The Bible constantly exhorts us to face the reality of conflict wherever it exists. The prophet Jeremiah complained about those who blandly said 'Peace, peace, when there is no peace'.[4] We must face up to the situation as it really is and not proclaim a false peace. It is not a Christian solution to pretend that conflict does not exist and it certainly is not the way of Jesus Christ.

Nor is it Christian to deny the reality of the human aggressive instinct and to adopt an entirely passive approach, even in the face of evil. Dr Norman Pittenger once said, 'There is nothing Christian in saying I am a doormat, please walk on me'.[5]

Christian hymn books are full of hymns urging us to 'Take up the Cross', and 'Fight the good fight'. Yet the secret of true reconciliation of conflict is NOT for one side simply to 'flatten' the other side so that they feel that they have lost everything. The secret of true reconciliation is not to produce what those engaged in negotiation call 'win-lose' situations. The secret of true reconciliation is to produce the kind of effective compromise that enables both sides to emerge from the conflict with some pride and heads held high. It is sometimes not easy to enable Christians to accept the idea of compromise. Yet responsible compromise (as opposed to irresponsible compromise) is more likely to be in tune with Biblical insights and teaching about the need to love our neighbour.

The whole idea of conflict is one of the major themes of the Bible. There is a great deal of discussion in the Bible about conflict in work situations. In the Old Testament the book of Deuteronomy discusses many aspects of work values.[6] In the New Testament, Jesus described the sort of things that happen when people disagree about wages, for example when asked to work in vineyards.[7] Whilst this particular parable ought not to be used to pontificate on all aspects of wage bargaining (for it was not intended for that purpose) it does however illustrate how one principle (fair wages for a fair days work) can be balanced against another principle i.e. the need for everybody to feel loved, wanted and valued and to have a special place in the vineyard. That is what the Kingdom of God is all about. There is a place for everybody in God's kingdom. We do not have to be justified by our work!

Conflict in the Bible is basically between good and evil, life and death, light and darkness.[8] Moreover the Bible teaches that all creative conflict involves sacrifice. Conflict inevitably involves those engaged in it making major personal sacrifices. Moreover Christian sacrifice embraces love. Jesus reveals a quality of love which even death could not defeat.

> 'Death's mightiest powers have done their worst
> And Jesus hath his foes dispersed'[9]
> 'Love's redeeming work is done;
> Fought the fight, the battle won.'[10]

Conflict can sometimes be demonic. Christian love demands that we take conflict very seriously even though it might mean the ultimate in sacrifice. This reaches its culmination in the sacrifice that Jesus himself made on the cross. That was the ultimate cost of reconciling the cosmic conflict between the forces of good and the forces of evil. Moreover, from that ultimate sacrifice can emerge resurrection and new life. That is the heart of the Christian gospel and it is the ground of our hope for the future. For although Christ's reconciling work, culminating in his crucifixion at a particular point in human history, effected a reconciliation that has cosmic and global dimensions, it can be equally effective for ALL time, both in specific social and specific individual conflict situations here and now. And that includes conflict at the work-place!

One of the most important texts for those who work at the 'front line' is from one of St Paul's letters to the Church at Corinth:

'God was in Christ reconciling the world to himself, and he has entrusted to US a ministry of reconciliation.'[11] That is our task as Christians at the front line, not as it were to save brands from burning but in the full sense of effecting reconciliation within each situation where conflict becomes demonic.

'Incarnation', 'resurrection' and 'reconciliation' are key words for Christians involved in conflict situations at the front line. Another Biblical word that is also of great importance is 'forgiveness'.

Forgiveness

Forgiveness is all about the healing of disunity through the atoning work of the one God – Father, Son and Holy Spirit.

God is Trinity in Unity and his purpose is to bring unity to mankind and to his world.

'The Lord our God is one Lord, and you shall love the Lord your God with all your heart and with all your mind and with all your soul and with all your strength and you shall love neighbour as yourself.'[12] When we worship the one true God we are committing ourselves to a continual attitude of forgiveness to those around us. It is the worship of idols (and there are many forms of idolatry today) that leads to disunity.[13] The God revealed in Jesus Christ takes the initiative in offering forgiveness. The father in the story of the prodigal son is pictured as running to meet the boy, throwing his arms round him and embracing him in his family when his son returns home. He kills the fatted calf for him in spite of all he has done.[14]

Modern examples may appear to be more difficult to relate to these parables. 'British Airways versus Virgin Atlantic' and 'The Miners versus the Government' provide two very different modern examples. The miners' strike was a most bitter and prolonged dispute with the Government of the day. The Airways dispute was equally bitter in a different sort of way! In January 1993 Virgin Atlantic received compensation from British Airways for illegal computer hacking on a gigantic scale. Virgin Atlantic passengers had been 'poached' by BA representatives who told them (wrongly) that flights had been cancelled.

These are two very different examples of acrimonious conflict in the front line of the market place. Sometimes situations of conflict in commerce and industry can be so deep that forgiveness becomes almost impossible. Can there be forgiveness between the miners and Mrs Thatcher? Can there be forgiveness between Virgin Atlantic and British Airways?

Yet forgiveness is as relevant in those situations as it was between Britain and Germany after the Second World War. In the midst of that war, which involved the destruction of the Cathedral Church of St Michael in Coventry, England (and Cathedrals in Germany!), the Christian community in Coventry inscribed on the charred altar in the ruins of the Cathedral the words:

'Father forgive.'

This was not intended to mean, 'Forgive those Germans for doing this dreadful deed of destruction' but 'Forgive us ALL for we are ALL part of this warring humanity'.

After the war further words were inscribed which made it clear that Christians in Coventry believed that their Cathedral Church was both BURNT and REBUILT to the glory of God. That Cathedral, whose ministry of reconciliation is symbolised by a cross made out of charred beams and medieval nails, developed a ministry of reconciliation within industry and commerce in the city of Coventry. I was privileged to be part of that Cathedral team and I shall always treasure those years of my ministry.

I end this chapter by quoting some words which sum it all up:

FATHER FORGIVE

The hatred which divides nation from nation, race from race, class from class
Father, forgive
The covetous desires of men and nations to possess what is not their own
Father, forgive
The greed which exploits the labours of men and women and lays waste the earth
Father, forgive
Our envy of the welfare and happiness of others
Father, forgive
Our indifference to the plight of the homeless and the refugee
Father, forgive
The lust which uses for ignoble ends the bodies of men and women
Father, forgive
The pride which leads us to trust in ourselves, and not in God
Father, forgive.

(The Coventry Litany of Reconciliation)

CHAPTER FIFTEEN

Training for the Front Line

Military Training

I cannot claim to have served in the front line of a fighting regiment in war time but I can claim to have received military training! I served two years National Service in the Royal Air Force as an Air Wireless Mechanic. My training consisted of two parts. First there were eight weeks of vigorous recruit training with lots of 'square-bashing' to convert me from a raw civilian into a fighting man. Next followed six months of intensive training to enable me to service wireless sets in a variety of military aircraft. This training was extremely important. Human lives depended on efficient wireless communication from ground-to-air and air-to-air. So the equipment that I was trained to service had to function properly. I was also trained to service 'A.Y.F.', a sophisticated radio altimeter upon which pilots depended to enable them to calculate their height from the ground.

The training which I received in the Royal Air Force was highly functional. It was geared to very specific tasks. In the course of recruit training, for example, with the aid of sacks stuffed with sawdust, we were trained to kill the enemy with a bayonet. I can vividly recall being trained to charge with my bayonet at full speed into a stuffed sack swinging from a piece of rope, urged on by the ferocious oaths of the corporal: 'Go on, you silly little man, kill him – in – out YAH!'

However, in addition to training, the Royal Air Force also provided 'education' for an hour or two each week. This was quite different. It was considered by some to be something of a 'skive'! We were marched off to the 'Education Centre'. There we had the opportunity to listen to lectures, read books, listen to music – all designed to develop the mind and lift the spirit. Our 'education' period also enabled us to reflect upon the training we received.

The 'Church Centre' (another opportunity to 'skive'?) was adjacent to the 'Education Centre'. Perhaps it was no accident that during my two years National Service I discovered my call to become a priest!

Training and Education

After National Service I embarked on training for the priesthood in the Church of England. It took some time before I realised that I was not in fact being 'trained' for the priesthood at all! Theological 'training' is a misnomer. I was being theologically 'educated'! Training and education are not the same thing.

This is an important point. At the time of writing it is thirty four years since I left theological college and it seems to me that the Church of England has still not fully learnt the difference between training and education. Of course there are notable exceptions but, by and large, the Church of England 'educates' people to become priests. Very little is done in theological colleges to prepare students for the actual day-to-day tasks that priests of the Church of England have to undertake. How are they to deal with drop-outs, addicts, beggars and homeless people? How are they to administer a full chalice without spilling it and perform the thousand and one daily demands upon a priest including the important task of being sensitive and supportive to lay people in their front line activities? Principals of theological colleges seem to be under great pressure from academic institutions to prepare students for examinations. External people (such as industrial chaplains) have to 'plead their cause' alongside a host of other demands for input into the curriculum!

The result is that when these students are ordained and become responsible for devising training courses for lay people, the emphasis again seems to be focused on academic type lay education rather than training lay people for ministry in their areas of secular responsibility. A recent course of basic lay 'training' in one Diocese consisted of Old Testament and New Testament studies, Christian Doctrine, Church History and a study of the lives of some of the Saints. Very little help was given in applying Christian insights and Christian faith to the daily secular tasks that lay people encounter 'at the front line'.

That is not to say that theological education is unimportant nor to say that educating lay people in biblical studies and other academic matters is of low priority. Indeed theological education is of the greatest importance. But it needs to be applied and lay people should be trained to 'theologise' about the practical real life issues that they actually face every day. What seems to be lacking in the Church of England (and this is true of most Churches) is an appreciation of the importance of training for specific tasks. The Church should perhaps take training at least as seriously as the Royal Air Force undertakes its training programmes! Training is task-centered. Whether our task is to nail two pieces of wood together, repair a radio, operate a computer or drive a motorcar, specific training is required in order to carry out the task successfully. In contrast, education is person-centred. Education is designed to develop the human potential to the full – body, mind and spirit. The word education is derived from the latin word *e-ducere*, meaning to lead out. Education brings out the full human potential and is complementary to training. A person with a broad based education is probably more able to be trained and retrained throughout life to carry out a multiplicity of different tasks.

Tasks at the Front Line

From the stories told earlier in chapter four, as well as from listening to many other stories, it would seem that there are two types of tasks that lay people undertake at the front line.

Firstly there are the 'professional' tasks to perform for which people are paid. This is true whether they are bus drivers, accountants, factory managers or politicians. They are required to be professionally competent. A 'Christian' accountant has to be trained to be at least as professionally competent as a non-Christian accountant. It is no use employing an accountant just because he is a Christian if he is incompetent! This perhaps may appear to be obvious, but frequently Christians are employed or engaged by clients simply because they are Christians and sometimes their professional competence is lacking.

So the first task is to ensure training in professional competence. It is beyond the scope of this book to make any further recommendations on this matter! We shall concentrate on the second matter:

Secondly there are those tasks which involve coming to grips with the (sometimes) alien value systems, strains and stresses which surround Christian people as they engage in their 'professional' tasks. Young people particularly find this difficult when they finish their 'professional' training and start work. For example they need to know how to relate to people in senior positions as well as to those junior to them, how to cope with sexism, ageism or racism and how to cope with the dishonesty which may surround them at work.

Post Ordination Training: 'Shadowing'

In view of what has been said about ministerial training at theological colleges perhaps one of the most important tasks for the Church is to ensure that ordained ministers are given insights into the 'world at the front line' during Post Ordination Training programmes and subsequent training programmes on offer to ordained ministers throughout their career.

Industrial Missions can offer their expertise for this purpose. One possibility is to set up opportunities for ordained ministers to 'shadow' lay people in their front line duties. For this to be effective it is important that the ordained minister who decides to accept this opportunity, sets aside as a matter of priority one day per week or one week a year (or whatever the arrangement may be) and adhere to the 'shadow' commitment in a disciplined manner. Nothing, other than extreme emergencies, should interfere with that priority to be at the front line, in a factory, city town hall, office, railway station or wherever the person being shadowed is working.

The opportunity given to ordained ministers to shadow

lay people at the front line should be followed up by discussion both with the person shadowed and in the context of the kind of support groups described elsewhere in this book. This kind of 'shadowing' exercise has a two-way benefit both for ordained ministers and the lay people involved. It informs ordained ministers and it demonstrates to the lay people concerned that their lay ministry is being taken seriously by the Church.

Training Lay People for their Front Line Tasks

'Shadowing' provides a practical opportunity for lay people to 'tell their story' and to identify potential areas of conflict and stress and therefore identify their training needs. It also provides opportunity for lay people to be empowered with spiritual, ethical, biblical and theological 'equipment' for their everyday tasks.

Shadowing may lead to the setting up of a network of support groups and training projects of the kind initiated by Industrial Mission in the Diocese of Peterborough and by the William Temple Foundation in Manchester.

Conflicting Values

Rachel Jenkins in her paper entitled *Changing Times, Unchanging Values* describes a project which attempted to offer training to Christian lay people in Manchester who were experiencing a mismatch between the characteristic values of their faith and those values prevalent at work.[1]

'The publicity invited people to participate who were in danger of losing their jobs, or doing what was expected and losing their self respect. They were invited to form a resource group.

The first task with the newly formed group was to establish trust between members. This was approached partly by sharing information about their work but mainly by agreeing together a set of ground rules by which the group should be conducted.

First of all it was agreed that the group should not expect to find consensus on every single issue discussed but rather to explore the understanding and experience that each person brought. Each person's experience was to be respected as genuine and valid. A rule of confidentiality was accepted.

The next stage was analysis. Values held by members of

the group were identified. The process revealed inconsistencies between belief and practice. These values were then compared with the values of employing organisations.

Participants became able to identify areas in their organisations where they realistically did have some influence, they became able to identify other people in the organisation whose interests coincided with their own and they became able to understand what constraints they were under.

In working towards the planning of strategic action it was recognised that attention should be paid to those skills which participants lacked.'

Rachel Jenkins states that during these meetings two important questions emerged firstly concerning the development of a spirituality which makes impact upon structures and secondly recognising the apparent powerlessness in which many people find themselves. The group identified the need to develop a spirit of 'unquiet endurance'.

From School to Work – Learning to Earning

The transition from school to employment has already been mentioned. The transition from learning to earning can be both exciting and frustrating for young people – that is if they are lucky enough to be able to find employment!

A number of organisations, such as The Industrial Society work alongside the Church in assisting young people to cope with the transition from school to work. Industrial Chaplains frequently arrange 'Learning to Earning' courses and conferences. These consist of both day courses and longer residential courses.

The Industry Churches' Forum has produced an excellent training pack for young adults entitled *People at Work*. It is an exciting training programme full of practical things to do and to discuss. The training pack tackles a number of issues including Working Together, Relationships at Work, Equality at Work, Honesty at Work, Trade Unions and Work and Leisure. The training pack contains sample interviews and role play material and sets out ways in which young people may 'shadow' more senior executives along the lines described elsewhere in this chapter.

Centres for Ethics and Social Policy

Britain may have something to learn from some of the lay training establishments which have been set up recently in America and in Australia. I have already described the Centre for Ethics and Social Policy in Berkeley and the Vesper Society located in San Leandra in California. In Sydney, Australia, The Society of Certified Practising Accountants has added ethical counselling to its list of membership services, following a spate of instances where accountants have 'bent' corporate accounts to the whim of strong-willed managers. The ethics centre is located in St James' Church and is known as the St James' Ethical Centre. Accountants who turn to the centre for help are talked through a step-by-step process that includes a discussion of their own ethical principles and the events which gave rise to their dilemma. Step by step they are assisted towards finding constructive solutions. In view of the accountant's story in chapter four and in the light of revelations about Robert Maxwell's activities, St James' Centre could well become a model to be replicated in commercial and financial centres throughout Britain![2] One such centre which is already well established in Britain is the William Temple Foundation in Manchester.

The William Temple Foundation

Before moving to Manchester the William Temple College was located in Rugby. I have vivid memories of the Rugby days when the college Principal was Mollie Batten a formidable and wonderful lady, fond of smoking a pipe! The courses which she ran for lay people from all professions were superb. Few of those who participated were active members of church congregations, but nearly all were keen to relate Christian insights to their daily work. Mollie did not hesitate to expound those great themes of St Paul: integrity, faith, salvation, spirit – in practical down to earth ways which related to the experience of those who attended. Mollie Batten used to describe her courses[3] 'primarily as an endeavour in the theological education of the "laos" (laity). The aim is that each student may grow in ability to understand their faith and to "theologize" in an informed and articulate way about their concern in the world and particularly in their vocation'. The William Temple Foundation in Manchester continues Mollie's tradition.

Coping with Stress

We have already seen in a previous chapter that many people (not just Christians!) find it difficult to cope with stress at work. It is possible to set up training programmes to deal with these kinds of problems. Examples include:

1. *Stress Awareness Workshops*

These can be run as 'one-offs' or as part of a programme. Stress awareness workshops aim not only to help in the recognition and understanding of stress in the individual but also to be aware of stress in colleagues and subordinates.

2. *Counselling*

Some companies in the United Kingdom have introduced employee helplines or confidential counselling services. Some companies employ their own in-house counsellor or use the service of an industrial chaplain. Co-counselling described in chapter ten can be taught.

3. *Relaxation Techniques*

Relaxation techniques can be taught on an individual or group self help basis. It should be noted, however, that whilst people do experience relief of stress symptoms through relaxation and massage, the root cause of the stress may be left untouched. The causes of stress within institutions should also be tackled (see chapter nine).

4. *Meditation*

There are various forms of meditation for which training courses are available. An article in *The Times* (17 February 1973) described the technique used in this way: 'The meditator sits with eyes closed and focuses his attention on an internally repeated "mantra" until the mind becomes still. (A powerful Christian mantra is the name "Jesus"). In this state of stillness the activity of the nervous system is altered in such a way that the stresses of living are neutralized and the creative energy of the individual is recharged.'

Equipment for the Front Line Tasks

Soldiers at the front line in battle are equipped for their task. In modern times this equipment is very sophisticated. In New Testament times the soldiers' equipment was comparatively simple.

Just as soldiers at the front line need equipment for the battle so likewise Christian Lay People require equipment to cope with the battles against alien values, stress and other conflicts.

St Paul knew all about front line ministry. By tradition St Paul earned his living as a tentmaker. He also knew all about the equipment needed by soldiers at the front line, no doubt by studying the soldiers who guarded him in prison.

In his letter to the Ephesians he describes a soldier's equipment:

'Put on the full armour provided by God, so that you may be able to stand firm against the stratagems of the devil ... fasten on the belt of truth, for a breastplate put on integrity; take up the shield of faith ... accept salvation as your helmet, and the sword which the spirit gives you, the word of God.' (Ephesians ch 6 v 11–17).

There is a wide range of equipment available for Christian lay people at the front line. Essential items mentioned by St Paul in the passage quoted above are: integrity, faith, salvation and the empowerment provided by God's Holy Spirit. But other items include the Bible, theological insight and prayer. The importance of setting aside time to enable lay people be trained to use this equipment cannot be overstated! Many of the centres mentioned in the appendices to this book provide training in the use of St Paul's list of equipment.

In the Selly Oak Colleges, for example, Ian Fraser pioneered exciting methods of Bible study gathering around him the most extraordinary groups from industry and commerce, mainly from among the trade unions. He had the great gift of demonstrating the relevance of the Bible in a 'secular' style.

The Bible: Bible Workshops

Ian Fraser describes his training methods in his book *Re-inventing Theology as the People's Work*:

'People are encouraged to get into a Bible passage themselves by relating to some element within it in terms of their own experience or attitude or feelings. It is necessary at an early stage in a Bible Workshop that people should feel that they are genuinely part of the story in the Bible passage and not merely "students" of the story. This can be done by role play.

> How does the story (or passage) connect with your own
>   experience?
> What bells does it ring in your memory?
> Are there problems for you in this passage?
> Is it offensive to you in any way?
> With which characters can you identify?
> What does it feel like to be that character?
> What message or mandate do you get from the passage?'

Fraser says:[4]

'It is necessary to make it clear that we are going to the biblical material to gain resources so as to enable us to be more effective as agents of the Kingdom of Christ to which the Gospel testifies. We are not interested in this material simply as "students". We are "trainees" seeking resources for a job which is laid upon us.'

Trainees are encouraged by Ian Fraser to use the Bible as a vital piece of equipment in their front line ministry.

Theology

In the same book Ian Fraser encourages trainees to regard THEOLOGY as an important item of equipment.

He writes:[5]

'Theology for living cannot be got from books ... Theology is for those who fly. Its quality must be decided, corrected, verified by those who take the risk of leaving safe ground ...'

In his book Fraser describes theological workshops run with managers and shop stewards as they grappled with real life issues such as such as the role of multi-national companies and of combine committees.[6]

Training in Prayer

Prayer is a vital item of equipment. Training in prayer has always been regarded as a high priority by the Church and so much has been written on this subject. St Paul says:

'Constantly ask God's help in prayer, and pray always in the power of the spirit. To this end keep watch and persevere, always interceding for all God's people'.[7]

A selection of books which deal with training in prayer can be found in the bibliography. Here I simply want to make a few general observations.

We have already seen in the chapter on spirituality that it is important to give people permission to pray, with little or no boundaries to their spirituality. This may appear an odd thing to say but the mere fact that some of the verses in the psalter have been 'put in brackets' suggests that there are certain 'feeling prayers' that are deemed to be not permissible for Christians in some traditions. The result is that some people may be inhibited from expressing their deepest thoughts and feelings to God. They are unable to 'off-load' all the stresses and strains of their life on to God. Their spirituality may therefore lack complete authenticity. Instead of allowing Jesus Christ to liberate them from feelings of guilt they may become even more burdened by guilt feelings. I emphasise again therefore that it is all right to bring to God our anger, our fears, our temptations our frustrations and our conflicts as well as our joys and our successes. God affirms us 'just as we are'. We do not have to hide part of our true situation from Him. The first and perhaps the most basic aspect of training in prayer for the front line is to support and encourage people in their quest for an authentic spirituality – a spirituality which they can 'own' rather than a spirituality that is false or phoney or which is imposed upon them!

Prayer Workshops

One way of providing this training is through prayer workshops. Such workshops do not consist of lectures or addresses by 'spiritual masters' but rather provide opportunity for a candid exchange of experiences and confessions. By this I do not mean hearing confessions of sin (though this may be included) but giving people the opportunity to talk about their prayer life in an open and honest way and so to jettison some of the burdens which may have been imposed upon them. Some of the 'rules of life' accepted by lay people with the best of intentions have only added to (instead of reducing) those burdens.

The second point which I wish to underline is the deep yearning after spiritual things which I detect in a wide cross section of people who may have abandoned traditional religion. This is so particularly among young people who seek to 'switch on' to things beyond themselves, albeit by the use of drugs. There is a growing realisation that material goods cannot satisfy spiritual needs. Maslow and other Behavioural Scientists, such as Frederick Hertzberg, have shown that there is a hierarchy of human needs ranging from the purely physical (which need to be satisfied by material means) through the social needs, to the highest needs for human self fulfilment. Prayer workshops can encourage people to explore beyond traditional boundaries. Indeed, the question arises is it possible to draw a line between spirituality and life? *Laborare est Orare*. To work is to pray!

This leads to my third point which is to encourage people, in prayer workshops, to discern the presence of the risen Jesus and the work of the Holy Spirit in day-to-day secular life. Jesus promised that he would, after his resurrection, go ahead of the disciples into Galilee (Matthew 28 v 10). Galilee was the place where most of his disciples worked, as fishermen or in other 'trades', and so Galilee therefore represents the 'front line'.

As we have already seen, the 'front line' is, almost by definition, a place of conflict and stress. Jesus himself experienced conflicts of various kinds in Galilee, even with his own kith and kin. Yet the image of Galilee that we sometimes have in our minds is a place of peace and calm :

> 'O Sabbath rest by Galilee,
> O calm of hills above,
> Where Jesus knelt to share with thee
> The silence of eternity
> Interpreted by love . . .'[8]

However Galilee is only 'calm' because Jesus kneels in its midst. We need to assist people in three tasks: to identify signs of the calming influence of Jesus in the midst of the front line conflicts, to discern the saving work of Jesus in the midst of their secular life and to taste the fruits of His spirit (love, joy, peace, justice, goodness) in those places where they spend most of their working lives.

'Drop Thy still dews of quietness,
Till all our strivings cease . . .'⁹

The Shield of Faith

St Paul tells us that faith is a vital item of equipment at the
front line. Faith is an ambiguous word. It can either mean a set
of beliefs or it can mean trust. It is one thing to believe that a
chair exists, it is an entirely different matter to believe (i.e.
trust) that the same chair will bear our weight when we sit
upon it.

Both meanings of the word are important for the Christian
at the front line. People generally act according to what they
believe to be true. If we seek to change a person's behaviour it
is necessary, first to change what they believe. If we are
seeking to encourage high standards of ethics in business life it
is important to help business people to believe that 'Good
Business' can be profitable. Strategies for changing human
behaviour (for example, away from exploitation of poorer
countries) must include changing beliefs, appealing to the best
in people and containing the worst excesses of human greed.
This has great significance for the Decade of Evangelism!

But faith means more than simply a set of beliefs. Faith
also means trust . . . in Christ. Trust in Christ in the midst of
the conflicts at the front line.

No single workshop can provide such training. Such faith
can only be learnt in the workshop of life. Some people would
argue that such faith is an anchor point for Christians at the
front line. In the midst of sweeping changes all around, Christians are secure in the presence of the unchanging Christ. I
myself find this to be a little over simplistic. Christians are
called by God to mature faith. Is it right to teach that the
Christian faith will provide an anchor point in every circum-
stance? Perhaps the truer meaning of 'faith' is learning to live
without an anchor! Faith is not the same thing as certainty.
There can be no belief without the possibility of unbelief!

In Galilee, Jesus challenged his disciples to 'Launch out
into the deep'. Jesus makes the same challenge to us today.

CHAPTER SIXTEEN

Liturgy and Worship for the Front Line

Norwyn Denny, writing in a pamphlet for the Westhill College programme for 'Christians in Public Life'[1] points out that Liturgy, (another name for the structure of worship) began as a declaration in public of beliefs held in private. It is a 'coming out' into the public sphere of beliefs held in private. She says that what still needs to be maintained in worship is this aspect of publishing abroad our belief in God, and our response to God's world.

'Unfortunately', she says, 'Religion is often thought to be what you do in the private realm. The criticism about "keeping politics out of it" are about keeping worship in the private "spiritual" realm. Nothing could be more destructive. For if worship does not touch, encounter and invade, every aspect of life, then it is neither true worship nor rooted in true Christian community. The structure of liturgy is determined by our approach to God and to the whole of his creation.'

The same point was brought out in a rather different way by the *Worlds Apart* report quoted in the first chapter of this book. Businesses circulated in Surrey and Hampshire saw no role for the Church in the running of their affairs. The only exception to this position is where problems in the domestic and personal realms interfere with business efficiency. If, for example, marriage problems effect the productivity of workers, then the pastoral role of the Church may be relevant. In Surrey and Hampshire the Church was felt to have no role in normal day to day business life!

However, authentic worship is the public offering to God of the whole of life, both public and private, in adoration and praise. It is a public opportunity to ask God's forgiveness for all that is wrong and to seek Christ's salvation for ALL.[2]

> 'Almighty Father, who dost give
> The gift of life to all who live
> Look down on all earth's sin and strife
> And lift us to a nobler life.
>
> Hear thou the prayer thy servants pray
> Uprising from all lands today,
> And, o'er the vanquished powers of sin,
> O bring thy great salvation in!'

In worship we praise God publicly. We thank God for his many blessings. We bring before him in prayer all those who work, in the knowledge that in work, human beings have a share in God's ongoing creative activity. We dedicate to God our management of the earth's resources. We confess those things that are wrong and we seek salvation through Christ. Worship provides an opportunity to hear God's word and to receive the sacraments which enable us to be inspired and empowered for front line tasks.

For all this to be realistic and authentic, worship has to be 'earthed' in the real world as experienced by most people, and not just the world as seen through ecclesiastical spectacles. Herein lies the first difficulty.

What is the nature of the world portrayed by the Anglican Book of Common Prayer or for that matter The Alternative Service Book 1980 (ASB)?

The Book of Common Prayer portrays a pre-industrial revolution world, a world of a bygone age. A world in which 'man' (there is constant emphasis on the masculine gender!) has strayed from God's ways like 'lost sheep', a world where God fights on our side (even though we are 'miserable sinners') and a world where our duties to our neighbour (as set out in the Catechism) include submission to 'all governors, teachers, spiritual pastors and masters'. A catechist undertakes to 'order myself lowly and reverently to all my betters . . .'

The Anglican Book of Common Prayer was compiled in 1662. However, the Alternative Service Book (compiled in 1980) still speaks mostly in the masculine gender, still seems to be earthed in a pre-industrial age and makes little or no mention of daily work in commerce and industry except at the end of the service of Holy Communion where the congregation says:

> 'Send us out in the power of your spirit
> To live and work to your praise and glory.'

Whilst provision is made for Rogationtide (seed-time) and Harvest Festival, there is no provision in The Alternative Service Book for a festival of commerce and industry. Harvest Thanksgiving is still very popular, a time to affirm the work of the farming industry. St Luke's day provides an opportunity to pray for and to celebrate the healing ministry of doctors and nurses. However, no Sunday is set aside in the Christian calendar to celebrate and to pray for those who create wealth through economic activity, without which doctors and nurses cannot minister to the sick. In any revision of the ASB this surely must be a matter for urgent attention.

An Affirmation of Wealth Creation

Modern society depends for its very existence upon the wealth-creating activity of those who work in commerce and industry. Yet there is no regular official provision to celebrate and affirm those who undertake this vital activity.

Kenneth Adams, Comino Fellow of the Royal Society of Arts, speaking at a conference on Business Ethics said:

'Imagine a community which lived by fishing and then imagine that the community no longer celebrates the return of the ships with their catch, and no longer brings up its young people to recognise their dependence upon the work of their fishermen and no longer teaches its young people to fish. Such a community is doomed. It will become dependent upon the charitable gifts of other countries . . .'[3]

Britain lives by the economic enterprise of those who

work to create the nation's wealth in industry and commerce. Kenneth Adams went on to say:

'The affirmation and celebration of the essential good- ness of the task of creating wealth, in order to provide the essential materials required to feed, house, clothe and care for the community, should be built into our regular Sunday worship.'

The question of wealth creation is the subject of some debate. The Bishop of Oxford's book on this subject[4] is a book that all should read who wish to pursue this matter at greater depth. It is possible to be too simplistic, and business people tend to be very sensitive to the Church's criticism of business life, as was clearly demonstrated following a sermon on the subject by the Archbishop of Canterbury.[5]

Kenneth Adams does not deny that there are sinful busi- ness people as there are sinful fishermen, sinful farmers, sinful doctors, sinful nurses and sinful clergy! Yet he maintains that the fundamental task of economic activity (without which no social services can be provided) is itself ethical and should be affirmed in worship. This affirmation is at the heart of the Christian Gospel and is at the heart of worship for the front line. 'God loves the world so much that he gave his only son Jesus Christ for the world.'

There are, however, very few books with liturgies, prayers and resource materials to assist those who wish to celebrate industrial festivals, commercial successes or techno- logical achievements, apart from Cameron Rutland's compila- tion called *Work in Worship*. Industrial Missions and organi- sations such as The Industrial Society and the Industry Churches' Forum have produced various order papers, but these do not seem to have filtered through to the main stream of public worship. Norwyn Denny reminds us that, 'Worship must touch, encounter and invade' every aspect of life if it is to be real'.[6] This is a difficult and time-consuming task. Later in the chapter I shall return to a discussion of practical ways in which this might be done in formal worship, but first I want to discuss less formal ways of worship and alterna- tive ways of 'being the Church'. If the 'Worlds Apart' gap is to bridged, more than one type of bridge may need to be built!

Holy Communion

The central act of Christian worship is the service of Holy Communion. If Holy Communion is to be both 'holy' and 'communion' it should reflect an authentic communion between Almighty God, creator of the universe, and the world which he has created. The act of communion must 'touch and invade' every aspect of the lives of the worshippers. It should be an act of 'holy bridgebuilding'.

In many of the formal acts of Holy Communion which take place in traditional church buildings this 'bridgebuilding' may not happen. Indeed there may not even be authentic communion between the officiating minister and members of the congregation. This lack of communion may occur for a variety of reasons. It is not easy to devise an order of communion with sufficient flexibility for general use. Some time ago, a group of industrial chaplains did make an attempt to devise, with the help of a group of lay people, a 'simple act of communion' for informal occasions. The order was eventually published by the Daily Bread Co-operative in Northampton. We produced the order as a response to our conviction that worship should grow out of our day to day life as Christians, with colleagues at work as well as friends and family at home.[7]

Industrial Missions have also pioneered a variety of ways of being the Church which do not involve large formal church buildings. Examples include informal 'supper' groups, workplace groups, business breakfasts, 'pub' groups, etc. In one 'pub group', the parish priest, who was also an Industrial Chaplain was able to relate to a group of men in a local public house in a way in which he could never relate to members of his congregation in a more formal act of worship. There was a real sense of 'communion' over a 'pint', a deep sense of mutual concern, and a concern for the wider community. Although the question may be asked 'But was it holy?!' industrial chaplains are able to build up deep relationships of trust with groups of people at workplaces, in businesses and in trade union networks. They do so, not by convening special services or Christian 'cells' but by joining existing groups for 'communion' around the lunch table, board room, or mug of tea on the 'shop floor'. The Chaplain is able to explore with a wide variety of groups the relevance of Christian values and insights into specific economic issues. Sometimes, for example at Wates Ltd, the well-known building company, this has led to the breaking of the bread and the sharing of the cup at the workplace. If Holy Communion can be celebrated by troops in the trenches, why not at front lines in civilian life? Why not, indeed!

The question is sometimes asked, though this may be 'public' worship, is this valid worship and valid 'Church' or is it just 'extra mural' activity? It is traditionally held that the test of validity must be the breaking of bread and prayers (Acts 2 v 42), yet as we have seen in the chapter on spirituality, it is sometimes unwise to put too much insistence upon cultic acts. An essential aspect of Christianity is liberation from cultic acts! The symbols of bread and wine are not timeless nor universal. When a gang of drillers were invited to a service of Holy Communion using bread and wine, one of them described the experience as horrific . . . 'They spoke about drinking blood . . .' However a shop steward who was present said, 'This is what I stand for as well . . . sharing!' Clearly there are very wide culture gaps to be bridged.

I have already sounded a note of caution about cultic acts. Bonhoeffer wrote in his *Letters and Papers from Prison*: 'It is not some religious act that makes the Christian but participation in the sufferings of Christ in secular life.' However Bonhoeffer himself was a religious man who did not neglect Holy Communion. The truth, as so often seems to be the case, is of the 'both . . . and . . .' variety, namely, 'life for others and the breaking of bread and prayers.' Perhaps we should not define too closely the boundary posts of worship and where 'Church' becomes 'non-Church'.

Elements in Worship

All traditional definitions of worship seem to include the element of human beings 'relating to that which is of supreme worth'. For example, Bishop David Jenkins in his book *Living with Questions* says:

'Worship is attending to God. To join in worship is to join in the Church's attending to God. The practice of worship is essentially connected with the continuous grasp of the "otherness" of God.'

The difficulty is to effect authentic 'Holy Communion' between those who live in the REAL world and the God who is 'wholly other'. The numinous aspect of the Godhead must never be neglected or overridden by the informality of our worship.

David Jenkins has said that worship stands for the response to the supremely valuable, ultimately transcendent 'personalness', who is God. Worship directs us to the reality and worthwhileness of God as God. We are reminded by Anthony Bloom that it is impossible to worship God unless we are aware of the 'other'.

If God is 'wholly other', how can we relate to him in worship, yet alone have communion with Him? The phrases 'relate to' and 'aware of' seem to occur frequently in descriptions of worship. Human beings relate to each other, and to the world, through their five human senses – touch, taste, sight, smell, hearing. These five senses take on a new importance in the context of worship. Our relationship to God through the five senses is established through Jesus Christ Our Lord, who became Incarnate in the world and whose spirit touches and invades the world and upholds it in being from moment to moment. Our five senses are especially engaged in the sacrament of Holy Communion.

'Christ's touch has still its ancient power.'
'O taste and see how gracious the Lord is.'
'Come and see'.
'Wise men brought the gift of incense to the Christ child.'
'God spake the word and they were made. He commanded and they were created.'

Our five senses are part of our primal response to the universe and, through the universe, to our creator God, through Jesus Christ our Lord. It has always been part of traditional Christian culture to discipline our bodily senses (particularly during the season of Lent) in order to increase the sensitivity of our five senses towards one another and to God. Whilst we may not condemn such things as drink, sex, the motorcar and other pleasures of life, we would still want to stress the positive side of the need for human beings to maintain bodily health. This in itself is an important aspect of holiness. Perhaps the modern obsession for sport and the worship of sporting heroes is part of human striving for communion with God.

The use of silence is another important element of worship. Silence is one of the most basic primal elements in which human senses react, yet silence is sometimes very difficult to find and to sustain these days. This is reflected in the increasing popularity of fishing, gardening, 'retreats' (both sacred and secular), sailing, gliding, golf, sunbathing and walking. Perhaps we should encourage people to worship in their own way! There are common elements in all these ways of silent communing with nature. We are all bound up in the bundle of life together so it is not surprising to find common elements. As we become sensitive to nature and to life so we become sensitive to other people to and the OTHER in a wide range of human experience. To try to convert one group of people to another group's pattern of worship may invite disaster!

There are magic moments in life when we are given the privilege of the 'numinous' experience. Such moments may occur at an orchestral or choral concert. Music helps our worship to 'soar'. Or perhaps we may experience the awesome 'otherness' of God as we contemplate the beauty of nature or when we experience moments of silence.

There may be no need to prescribe a set pattern of worship. We do need, however, to start with the world (which God has created and in which Jesus Christ is Incarnate) and from this starting point become sensitive to the world as it IS through our five human senses. As we grow in sensitivity to the world around us so, (hopefully) we shall grow in sensitivity to the God who created the world. Rather than give people a traditional 'ready made' discipline of worship, perhaps we should help them to explore what IS. At times we may consciously put ourselves into situations in which an encounter with God can take place. This may happen in the silent place or at the workbench or anywhere amidst the conflicts at the front line. It may also happen during a formal act of worship in church.

To enable encounters with God in the world to be related to formal public worship, people at the front line should be given lots of opportunities to tell their own story. Some of the stories recorded in chapter four were told in the context of formal public worship.

For most people, the traditional formal act of worship in a formal and traditional church building is still the normal weekly experience. So we must ask how this formal liturgy and worship can be made real for those who minister as lay people at the front line. If the world of work and the Church's worship is (as the report stated) 'worlds apart', how can that 'apartness' be bridged? Norwyn Denny gives this advice:

'Those who accept the leadership of public worship should represent the whole Christian community. Worship should not be seen as something done "for" people at the front line, but should involve them and receive from them criticisms, comments, resources and any guidance they wish to offer. They may not be "professionals" in worship activity; they may not even wish to be further involved after their daily work in such activity; but they can be encouraged to speak their mind.'[8] That seems to be sound advice.

It is much easier and far less time consuming for ordained ministers to devise formal and traditional acts of worship without reference to lay people. The simplest method is to follow a set order and to adhere to the set lections. Yet experience over many years tells me that time spent in preparing worship, taking into consideration the needs of the congregation is time well spent. To do this effectively, members of the congregation, especially those with 'front line' tasks should be closely involved in the preparation work from the beginning. Each act of worship should have a theme with a very clear idea of what it is we wish to say to God. Each act of worship should be an opportunity to offer our lives in all their fullness to God. Each act of worship should uplift our hearts and minds, enlarge our vision and strengthen our faith. Such worship will liberate body, mind and spirit, and refresh, inspire and equip for service those who minister at the front line.

> 'Lift up our hearts, O King of Kings[9]
> To brighter hopes and kindlier things.
> To visions of a larger good,
> And holier dreams of brotherhood.
>
> Rejoice O land in God thy might;
> His will obey, him serve aright;

For thee the saints uplift their voice:
Fear not, O land, in God rejoice!'

PSALM 23 FOR BUSY PEOPLE
by Toki Miyashina

The Lord is my pace-setter, I shall not rush;
He makes me stop and rest for quiet intervals.
He provides me with images of stillness
Which restore my serenity.
He leads me in the ways of efficiency,
Through calmness of mind: and his guidance is peace.
Even though I have a great many things to accomplish each
    day
I will not fret, for his presence is here.
His timelessness, his all-importance will keep me in balance
He prepares refreshment and renewal
In the midst of activity.
By anointing my mind with the oils of tranquility,
My cup of joyous energy overflows.
Surely harmony and effectiveness
Shall be the fruits of my hours,
For I will walk in the pace of my Lord
And dwell in his house for ever.

(From a prayer leaflet on work compiled by Industrial Mission
                        in Hertfordshire and Bedfordshire)

CHAPTER SEVENTEEN

Epilogue

I end this book with another story from the front line. It is an edited extract from an address given by the Works Manager of a paint factory in Birmingham during a course given during Lent entitled 'Stories from the Front Line'. The person who gave this address is a regular member of the congregation of a city centre church in Birmingham. What he says is very important and seems to me to sum up so many of the issues discussed in this book.

A Manager at the Front Line

'What do we mean by the front line? I don't go to work in a tin hat and with a rifle! Some people see the front line as an area of confrontation and as part of a battle. I do not see my work as that. My work is difficult at times and pressurised, but I am, after all, a manager managing a production unit. I manage people. It is a job I like doing, and a job with God's help and with God's grace I feel I'm quite suited to do.

I'm a Christian doing a normal management job. But to me, being a practising Christian gives me that breadth of vision which helps me as I work with people. Management is often a difficult job. Last week our speaker said that we are social creatures and workers. My job is to weld the social and the work together and organise the work force so that people are satisfied in their work, and (most important) want to work with us.

People see their work in different ways and have a variety of attitudes towards it. There is the well known story about a visitor to a building site watching three men at work. The visitor asked what they were doing.

"Me?" said one. "I'm chipping stone".

"Me?" said another. "I'm earning £10 an hour".

"Me?" said the third man. "I'm building a Cathedral!"

I'm the Works Manager of a local paint factory. The factory where I work was started in 1881 by three brothers who started making black varnish for bicycles, bedsteads and umbrellas. During the Great War it made paints for munitions and then, between the wars, it became a major supplier of paint and varnish for railways and the motor industry. We are now part of a large multi-national company employing 35,000 people world wide. We supply surface coatings for the world's cars! We in Birmingham produce 18 million litres of our products every year and we have annual sales of £45 million. My job is to manage our production facilities to meet this demand.

What is the main objective of a company? One objective is to make a profit. But how does the main objective of making a profit fit in with the Christian ideal? Isn't profit sometimes a dirty word? Can one serve God and mammon?

Of course the real objective of a company is survival. We survive by making a profit. We employ people. We create jobs. We survive to create wealth. We are wealth producers.

The wealth we (and companies like us) create pays for our hospitals, education, social services, local government and welfare enabling the needy in our society to be cared for. I regard myself as part of the wealth creating process.

As a Christian, I see my job as Christian contribution to all this. I am building my own "Cathedral".

Wealth is produced by people. In industry there are two main elements: the "people" and the "process". The most important resource of any company is its people. Personnel Managers are no longer called "personnel". They are called "Human Resource Managers"! This is not a term that I like but I suppose it puts "people" in the right perspective.

I'm a factory manager. I have a number of key tasks. But the key part of my job is to manage "people" and "process". To me, being a practising Christian helps me do my job better because the commands to "love thy neighbour as thyself" and "do unto others as you would have them do unto you" are ideal work ethics. Put into practice they help to build up a trust. They help me to have empathy with people. Good relationships are built on mutual trust.

I started working for my present company thirty eight years ago. I've been a manager for over thirty years and a works manager for just over seventeen years. I count myself as an experienced manager. Throughout my time in industry I have seen many differences in management style. At one time a pat on the back was worth a pound in your pocket and the management were the "untouchables". Then came the time when union power was rampant and you really were in the front line then! There was much viciousness and divisiveness! Nowadays we are much smaller in numbers and there is a greater emphasis on team-work.

The paint trade is a highly competitive industry. My job, at times, is difficult. I have to meet production budgets, productivity goals, volume targets and cost budgets. I have to deal with machine breakdowns, union negotiations, redundancy proposals and crisis management. This often leads me to the prayer "If I forget Thee O God this day, please do not forget me". It is so easy sometimes to forget. I often wonder how much easier it would be to remember if I worked in the open air, on a farm or in a garden seeing things growing, seeing the trees and the sky and the wonders of nature. As we work hard to achieve results, so in turn, whatever our environment, we need to work hard to be Christians. To be a Christian is hard work!

I'm known as someone who regularly goes to Church. I'm known as a "Churchgoer"! Some use that as a derogatory term, I find that there is little to be claimed by being an overt evangelist in my work. This can turn people off! I believe that to be a Christian is to be happy and to show it. I tell myself, as a liberal Christian, "Lead by example". Work relationships are getting people to work WITH you, not "for" you. The future of our industries is working TOGETHER.

Every one, whatever his status, has a contribution to make. We are all given gifts to make that contribution. As St Paul writes in chapter 12 of his first letter to the Corinthians:

"There are varieties of gifts, but the same spirit. There

are varieties of service but the same Lord. There are varieties of work but in all of them and in all men the same God is active." It follows that whatever we do, and whatever we work at, all people should be given equal dignity.

One of the less skilled jobs in my work is the paint filler. He fills paint into cans at the end of the process. But the last person to handle the product before the customer is the paint filler so he is working on a very important job.

My industry is not labour intensive. We haven't vast numbers of workers. It is a chemical process industry. I feel, as Works Manager, that I should know the name of every person and know something about their interests and their families. This is not being intrusive. This is part of being able to relate to each them and they to me and is an important Christian principle.

One of the most frequent complaints within industry is about communication.

"The management doesn't communicate, the management doesn't know what's going on". There are many ways to communicate such as notices, meetings, magazines, briefing groups and so on, but you cannot beat the "face to face" meeting. I always make myself available to people. My office door is always open to any employee.

There are light moments in dealing with people and there are sad times. I go to all the funerals. It's no use saying that you care. You have to SHOW that you care, and give comfort.

Industry has gone through vast technological change in recent years. As technology improves and processes improve, fewer workers, especially manual workers, are required. Of course, office workers and accountants and even managers themselves are also affected. This is an area where the Church must help.'

The Challenge

I was immensely moved when I first heard that address. It presents an enormous challenge to enable the Church to support people who, like this Manager in the paint factory, work at the 'front line'.

By coincidence, as I reached the end of writing this book, there arrived through my letter box a publication from the General Synod of the Church of England entitled *Christian Education for the 21st Century*. The subtitle of the booklet is

'What are your priorities?'[1] The booklet asks a number of pertinent questions relevant to the subject of this book and underlines the increasingly high priority which the Church needs to give to supporting lay people in their public life. I was encouraged to note in a questionnaire on current issues that the very first question was 'Should we concentrate primarily on helping the gathered Church or in supporting "dispersed" Christians in their life in the world?' A further question was, 'Should adult education and training be focused on the individual or upon the individual within the community?' There needs to be a balance between supporting Christians in their front line activities and tackling issues raised by our works manager and other matters such as the impact of new technologies upon employment and the fabric of human society.

I hope that by focusing upon the role of lay people I have not given the impression that I undervalue the role of ordained ministers. Clearly, chaplains in secular institutions such as industry, universities, schools, the armed forces and prisons, exercise a front line ministry of immense importance. Likewise, Bishops who sit in the House of Lords and other senior ordained ministers such as the chaplain to the House of Commons, are in strong positions to influence 'principalities and powers'. Moreover ordained ministers in cities and towns (particularly in housing estates, inner city areas and other urban priority areas) have an extremely demanding ministry at the front line. They have their own support groups. A number of books have already been written about the ordained ministry in secular life. The present book specifically highlights the ministry of lay people.

Faced with ethical dilemmas, conflict, stress and other problems, those who exercise lay ministry at the front line may be tempted to 'give up' and 'get out'. Sometimes lay people may mistake their inability to reconcile Christian values with secular values as a Divine call to resign and seek ordination! This may sometimes be the right thing to do. God may indeed be calling more lay people to the ordained ministry. However, more often than not, God's call to lay people is to 'stay put'! This is what 'incarnation' is all about . . . staying in the thick of it! Although it may not always be easy to reconcile Christian values with secular values, some degree of responsible compromise is frequently necessary. Compromise is not always a dirty word. It may, for example, be more responsible for a Christian who is a director or a trade union official to stay at his or her post when beset by alien values and attempt to influence affairs from within, than to resign and opt out. Simon Phipps in his book *God on Monday* says: 'The Christian in public life can never do more than push public affairs slowly in a Christian direction. The speed with which Christians can do this may depend upon their realism about public affairs.'[2]

Simon Phipps frequently referred to what he called the 'zig-zag' approach. It is not always easy to head straight for the desired goal. A zig-zag approach may be the only feasible way forward. Sometimes we are in the 'zig' and sometimes we are in the 'zag' but we press towards the goal! This can produce a great deal of stress. Hence the importance of relevant support through prayer, worship and sensitive groups of people.

In the end, God Himself supports people at the front line but His presence is not always easy to discern. We have the assurance of the risen Jesus that, 'He goes ahead of His disciples into Galilee' (Matthew 28 v 10). Our Galilee is our secular activity. Wherever we go, wherever we work, whatever responsibility we have in public life, Jesus is with us, supporting us and ministering alongside us at the front line.

That is His promise.
That is the ground of our Christian faith.

Christ be with me,
Christ within me,
Christ behind me,
Christ before me,
Christ beside me,
Christ to win me,
Christ to comfort and restore me,
Christ beneath me,
Christ above me,
Christ in quiet,
Christ in danger,
Christ in hearts of all that love me,
Christ in mouth of friend and stranger.
I bind unto myself the name,
The strong name of the Trinity.[3]

Notes

Chapter 1

1. *Worlds Apart*: Report on a Survey by Surrey and Hampshire Industrial Mission.

Chapter 2

1. *The Monday Connection* William Diehl, page 12
2. Ibid.
3. *Mr Speaker* George Thomas, page 213
4. Colossians, ch 1 vv 15–20 (The Revised English Bible)
5. *Changing Times, Unchanging Values?* Rachel Jenkins. The William Temple Foundation. Reproduced with the kind permission of Rachel Jenkins.

Chapter 4

1. The House of Commons voted for partial de-regulation in December 1993 allowing large shops to open for six hours each Sunday and giving greater flexibility to smaller shops.

Chapter 5

1. *The Good Society* Robert Bellah, page 4
2. Similar programmes have been initiated in the Anglican Dioceses of Portsmouth and Guildford.

Chapter 6

1. The *Independent on Sunday* 3 January 1993
2. *The Monday Connection*. Diehl, page 43ff
3. Ibid, page 46
4. Ibid, page 97
5. *Changing Times, Unchanging Values?* Jenkins, page 18ff
6. Ibid, page 5ff
7. Ibid, page 10
8. Ibid, page 12
9. *Economic Justice for All* Pastoral Letter, page 1ff
10. Speech by President George Bush at Los Angeles, 8 May 1992

Chapter 7

1. Bill Jordan, now President of the Amalgamated Engineering and Electrical Union but at the time was Divisional Organiser in Birmingham.
2. *The Independent*, 4 March 1992
3. Ibid
4. Quoted in Personnel Management Fact Sheet No. 7, July 1988
5. *Managing Stress*, Ivor Capel and John Gurnsey. Constable 1988
6. See chapter 10 in this book
7. *The Independent*, 4 March 1992
8. A conference organised by the author in Coventry Cathedral

9. Ibid
10. Fact Sheet No. 7, July 1988
11. Hymn No.184. J.G.Whittier. *Hymns Ancient and Modern (Revised)*

Chapter 8
1. *The Monday Connection* Diehl, page 52ff
2. *The Gospel in a Pluralist Society*, Lesslie Newbigin, page 52
3. *Empowering the Laity*. Crabtree. The whole book is relevant!
4. Myers Briggs Type Indicator

Chapter 9
1. *The Good Society* Robert Bellah, page 4
2. Ibid, page 290
3. *Mainstream and Marginal*, Church of England Board of Social Responsibility, Chris Beales
4. Mission Statement. Cadbury Ltd. Reproduced with permission
5. Mission Statement. The Co-operative Bank plc. Reproduced with permission

Chapter 10
1. Details of co-counselling courses may usually be obtained from local libraries and colleges of education.

Chapter 11
1. Isaiah ch 1 vv 11–16
2. Psalm 43 v 5
3. Psalm 43 v 6
4. Hymn 298 *Hymns Ancient and Modern (Revised)*
5. Psalm 22 v 1
6. Psalm 43 v 6
7. Hymn 337 *Hymns Ancient and Modern (Revised)*
8. Desiderata. Thought to be Anon. and Found in Old St Paul's, Baltimore, USA. 1692
9. Most cities and towns have special support groups for gay people. Information about these groups can usually be obtained by telephoning Gay Switchboard.
10. Desiderata.
11. Hymn 349 *Hymns Ancient and Modern (Revised)*

Chapter 12
1. *Christianity and the Social Order* Archbishop William Temple, page 20 (Pelican)
2. *The Human Condition* Hannah Arendt, page 22
3. Ibid
4. Ibid
5. *Theological Word Book* A.Richardson, page 286
6. Deuteronomy 6 v 21
7. Hymn 133, *Hymns Ancient and Modern (Revised)*

8. *The Human Condition* Hannah Arendt, page 5
9. Ibid
10. Psalm 46 v 10
11. Hymn 336 *Hymns Ancient and Modern (Revised)*
12. *The Ideology of Work* P.D.Anthony, page 19
13. *The Protestant Work Ethic and the Spirit of Capitalism* Max Weber, page 177
14. Ibid
15. *The Ideology of Work* P.D.Anthony, page 43
16. Hymn 135, *Hymns Ancient and Modern (Revised)*

Chapter 13

1. *Time for a Rhyme* S.J.Forrest, page 7 (Mowbray)
2. *Work, Employment and the Changing Future* Denis Claringbull (Church of England Diocese of Birmingham)
3. The Church Action with the Unemployed. (c/o Elephant Jobs, 3 Stamford Street, London, SE1 9NT)
4. See chapter 12, pages 120–123

Chapter 14

1. Report on a statement by 'Liberty' in *The Independent* 12 January 1993
2. Tom O'Brien MP (a lecture given for the South London Industrial Mission)
3. Tom Lupton, from a lecture given in Coventry.
4. Jeremiah 6 v 14
5. Dr Norman Pittenger in an article in *The Times* 20 February 1971.
6. See Deuteronomy 14 vv 28–29; 15 vv 1–18; 24 10–15; 26 1–3, 12–13; etc
7. Matthew 20.
8. John 1 v 5.
9. Hymn No. 135, *Hymns Ancient and Modern (Revised)*
10. Ibid. Hymn 141
11. 2 Corinthians 5 v 19ff
12. Deuteronomy 6 v 5; Luke 10 vv 25–28
13. Psalm 106 v 19ff
14. Luke 15 v 11 ff

Chapter 15

1. *Changing Times, Unchanging Values* Rachel Jenkins, William Temple Foundation.
2. A centre for Business Ethics is being set up in the Birmingham City Centre.
3. *Theological Education* Vol LXVIII No 540 June 1965
4. *Re-inventing Theology as the People's Work*. Ian Fraser, page 58ff
5. Ibid, page 2
6. Ibid, page 64
7. Ephesians ch 6 v 18
8. Hymn 184, *Hymns Ancient and Modern (Revised)*
9. Ibid

Chapter 16

1. *Christians in Public Life* A position paper by Norwyn Denny. CIPL Programme Westhill College, edited by David Clark
2. Hymn 583, *Hymns Ancient & Modern (Revised)*
3. Birmingham Rotary Club, Good Business Conference 1991
4. *Is there a Gospel for the Rich?* Richard Harries, (Cassell 1992)
5. Sermon preached by Dr George Carey in Derby Cathedral May 1992
6. (see note 1)
7. *A Simple Communion* (Daily Bread Co-operative, 24 Weston Way Northampton. NN3 3BL)
8. (see note 1)
9. Hymn 582/583, *Hymns Ancient & Modern (Revised)*

Chapter 16

1. *Christian Education and Training for the Twentyfirst Century. What are your priorities?* Church of England GS MISC 389 (available from Church House Bookshop, Great Smith Street London SW1 3BN)
2. *God on Monday* Simon Phipps, page 104
3. St Patrick's Breastplate, Hymn 162, *Hymns Ancient and Modern (Revised)*

Bibliography

Background Reading

Habits of the Heart. Robert Bellah et al. (Harper & Row. USA)

The Good Society. Robert Bellah et al. (Alfred Knopf. New York)

New Patterns of Work. Ross. (St Andrew Press)

The Gospel in a Pluralist Society. Lesslie Newbigin. (SPCK)

The Gospel and Contemporary Culture. Edited by Montefiore. (Mowbray)

The Future of Work. Charles Handy. (Basil Blackwell)

Business Ethics

Good Business: A Guide to Corporate Responsibility and Business Ethics. Sheena Carmichael and John Drummond. (Hutchinson Business Books)

Ethical Issues in Business. John Donaldson. (Academic Press)

Groundwork of Christian Ethics. Richard Jones. (Epworth Press)

Business Morality. Peter Vardy. (Marshall Pickering)

Morality and the Market Place. Prof. Brian Griffiths. (Hodder and Stoughton)

Industry and Values. Michael Ivens. (Harrap)

Ethics, Environment and the Company. Tom Burke and Julie Hill. (Industrial Mission Association)

Corporate Strategy and the Search for Ethics. R.E.Freeman and D.R.Gilbert, Editors. (Prentice Hall)

Ethical Issues in Business. Thomas Donaldson and Pat Werhane. (Prentice Hall)

Business Ethics: 3rd Edition. R.T.deGeorge. (Macmillan USA)

Teaching Business Ethics. Jack Mahoney. (Athlone Press)

Ethics and Economics: A Christian Enquiry. Pat Wogaman. (SCM)

Greening Business. John Davis. (Blackwell)

The Changing of Corporate Values. (The Consumer Research Office)

Global Responsibility. Hans Kung. (SCM)

The Management of Values. Charles McCoy.(Centre for Ethics & Policy, Berkeley USA).

Economic Justice for All: Pastoral Letter on Catholic Social Teaching and the US Economy. (National Conference of Catholic Bishops Washington DC)

The Just Enterprize. George Goyder. (Andre Deutsch)

Company Philosophies and Codes of Business Ethics. (Institute of Business Ethics, 12 Palace Street, London SW1E 5JA)

Corporate Ethics, A Prime Business Asset. (The Business Round Table, 200 Park Ave., Suite 222, New York Ny 10166, USA)

The Ethics of Acquisitions (Church of England Board of Social Responsibility)

The Ethics of Investment and Banking. (The Church of Scotland, 120 George Street Edinburgh)

A Course in Business Ethics. [*The Jubilee Centre, Hooper Street, Cambridge*]

Good Business. A report of a Rotary Conference held in Birmingham. (Church House, 175 Harborne Park Rd, Birmingham B17 OBH)

The Moral Crisis in Management. (1967 McGraw-Hill Series in Management)

Theology

On Human Work (*Laborem Exercens*) Papal Encyclical 1981.

Contemporary Catholic Social Teaching. Relevant Papal Encyclicals. (National Conference of Catholic Bishops USA)

The Human Condition. Hannah Arendt. (University of Chicago Press)

Theological Word Book. A. Richardson (SCM)
Re-inventing Theology as the People's Work. Ian M. Fraser (USPG)

Lay Ministry in the Secular World

God on Monday. Simon Phipps. (Hodder and Stoughton)
Thank God it's Monday. William Diehl. (Laity Exchange Books, USA)
The Monday Connection. William Diehl. (Harper Collins, USA)
Laity Exchange. (The Vesper Society, San Leandra, California, USA)
God's Frozen People. Mark Gibbs. (Fontana Collins)
Work, Employment and the Changing Future. Denis Claringbull. (Church House, 175 Harborne Pk Rd, Birmingham B17 OBH)
The Greening of Accountancy. Robert Gray. (Dundee) (The Chartered Association of Certified Accountants. 29 Lincoln Inn Fields London WC2A 3EE)
Changing Times, Unchanging Values. Rachel Jenkins. (William Temple Foundation, Manchester)
People at Work: Thinking about Social and Moral Issues. (Industrial Christian Fellowship, [Now Industry Churches' Forum] 86 Leadenhall Street, London, EC3A 3DH)
The Christian in Industrial Society. H.F.R Catherwood (1964 The Tyndale Press)
A Survey of Christians at Work and its implications for the Churches. David Clark. (Nov. 1993) (Christians in Public Life Programme, Westhill College, Selly Oak, Birmingham, B29 6LL)

Liturgy and Spirituality

A Simple Communion. (Daily Bread Co-operative, 24 Weston Way, Northampton NN3)
Work in Worship. Cameron Butland. (Hodder & Stoughton)
Creative Ministry. Henri Nouwen. (A Doubleday Image book)

Organisations Offering Support and Expertise

Business Ethics (UK)

Industrial Mission Association, Business Ethics Network.

The Hinksey Centre, Westminster College, Hinksey, Oxford, OX2 9AT.

Institute of Business Ethics, 12 Palace Street, London, SW1E 5JA.

Christian Association of Business Executives. (As above)

London Institute of Contemporary Christianity, Dr Lucas, St Peter's Church, Vere Street, London, W1M 9HP.

The Institute of Directors, 116 Pall Mall, London, SW1Y 5ED.

Ethical Investment, Research and Information Service, Elliott Kendall, Room 401, 71 Broadway, London, SW8 1SQ.

Christian Ethical Investment Group, 43 Long Grove, Seer Green, Beaconsfield, Bucks, HP9 2YN.

Business Ethics Research Centre, Jack Mahoney, King's College, The Strand, London, WC1.

Christians Social Ethics Research Unit, The Reverend Francis McHugh, St John's Seminary, Wonersh, Guildford, GU5 0QX.

European Business Ethics Network, Dr Brian Harvey, University of Nottingham, University Park, Nottingham, NG72 2RD.

Corporate Community Relations International, David Logan, 10 Russell Street, Covent Garden, London, WC2B 5HZ.

Birmingham Business Ethics Centre, St Paul's Church, St Paul's Square, Birmingham, B3 1QZ.

Business Ethics (USA)

The Centre for Ethics and Social Policy (Also Bay Area Ethics Consortium), Bill Maier, Graduate Theological Union, Ridge Road, Berkeley, California.

The Vesper Society, 311 MacArthur Boulevard, San Leandra, California 94577.

Corporate Community Relations International, David Logan, 116 New Montgomery Street, Suite 220, San Francisco, CA 94105.

The Trinity Centre for Ethics and Social Policy, Dr David Schmidt, Trinity Church, Wall Street, New York.

American Enterprize Institute, Michael Novak, 1150 17th Street NW, Washington DC 20009.

Business Ethics (Europe)

UNIAPAC, Joseph Mertes, 2 Place des Barricades, B-1000. Brussels, Belgium.

Christians in Commerce, Industry and Public Life (UK)

Westhill College, Selly Oak, Birmingham, B29 6LL (Christians in Public Life Programme).

The Faith Business, Ridley Hall, Cambridge, CB3 9HG.

St George's House, Windsor Castle, Berkshire.

Industry Churches' Forum (ICF), 86 Leadenhall Street, London, EC3A 3DH.

The Industrial Mission Association. (Contact via Church House, Westminster, see below.)

The Church of England Board for Social Responsibility, Church House, Westminster, London, SW1.

William Temple Foundation, Manchester Business School.

Luton Industrial College.

The People and Work Programme, Diocese of Peterborough.

Survey Summary:
'CHRISTIANS AT WORK'
—and its implications for the Churches
by David Clark

100 pages of facts, figures, opinions and commentary
Published by Christians in Public Life
on 22nd November 1993

Origins

Early in 1993, **Christians in Public Life (CIPL),** a new Programme set up to support Christians active in public affairs and sponsored by Westhill College, Birmingham, undertook **a major enquiry** into **the experiences of Christians at work.** The aim was to discover in what ways Christians saw their faith influencing their working lives and how much help they got from their local churches in linking Sunday and Monday.

Nearly **400 people** representing all denominations and from across the country returned questionnaires. 60% were men and 40% women. Their ages ranged from under 30 to over 60. All but 31 were lay people.

Main findings

The survey produced **four major findings:**

- These Christians held influential positions and were deeply concerned to give meaningful expression to their faith in their working lives.

- They were strongly committed to and active in the life of their local churches.

- Their working lives and church lives were failing to connect – few were finding Sunday of any real use on Monday.

- They were willing to give time to meeting with others in order to get their faith and their working concerns more together.

In short, the enquiry revealed that **many Christians, influential in public life, are making every effort to relate their faith to their working lives but getting very little support from their local church in the process.**

A critical condition

With the latest census of church attendance showing a continuing decline in numbers, with an ageing membership and with its influence in the public arena steadily diminishing, such failure to equip and support its lay people in the thick of public affairs is both a denial of the church's missionary task and a sign of continuing attrition.

Any secular organisation faced with this situation would call an emergency meeting of its Board of Directors immediately!

Some other findings in more detail

- The survey showed that 92% of those replying saw their work as 'very much' or 'to some extent' a Christians vocation. 89% similarly saw their work as an integral part of the mission of the church.

- 7 out of 8 attended worship each Sunday. 75% held more than two church offices. 29% were lay readers or local preachers. As a whole they gave 4 hours per week to church affairs.

- **Overall, worship offered those replying only moderate help, pastoral care little, and education very little support in their working lives. Only a third of ministers or priests gave any real support to these Christians at work. The latter had only scant knowledge of what their fellow church members' occupations involved.**

- On these criteria of support, Methodists came off worst and Quakers best, but all denominations fared badly.

- Few of those replying had been able to use their occupational expertise or skills to enhance the life and work of the church.

- Over half of those replying were ready to give an evening a month to meet with others to talk over faith and work concerns. A third were keen to belong to some Christian group or association with an occupational focus.

Follow up by CIPL

Christians in Public Life was established in the spring of 1992. Since then the Programme has:

- produced over 50 Position Papers on related topics written by a range of prominent writers

- set up a network of Associates concerned to give more effective expression to faith in public affairs

- held a very successful first national conference in July 1993.

The Programme is Co-ordinated by the Revd Dr David Clark, a Methodist Minister and senior lecturer at Westhill College. It has a strong ecumenical Steering Committee.

This publication also reports on how CIPL is now set to launch **a follow**

up to its 'Christians at Work' enquiry. A major new project will be entitled **'Faith in Public Life'** and will consist of three years of action research with **two main fields of enquiry:**

- The setting up and/or support of a diversity of **forums** (groups, workshops, consultations, etc.) to discover how faith and public life can be related more creatively. These forums will be within secular institutions as well as the churches.

- Discovering from a sample of **local congregations** how public concerns can be more effectively brought into all aspects of their life and worship.

Resources are now being sought to get this Project underway.

'Christians at Work' is available from CIPL, Westhill College, Selly Oak, Birmingham, B29 6LL (Tel: 021–472 7245).
Cost (post paid): £19.50 (£14.50 CIPL Associates).
Cheques made out to **'Westhill College'** and sent to the above address.

Index